Made from scratch
PASTA

EVERYDAY
EASY
HOME
COOKING

This edition published by Parragon Books Ltd in 2014
LOVE FOOD is an imprint of Parragon Books Ltd

Parragon Books Ltd
Chartist House
15–17 Trim Street
Bath BA1 1HA, UK
www.parragon.com/lovefood

ISBN 978-1-4723-2993-6

Printed in China

Cover photography by Ian Garlick
New photography by Clive Bozzard-Hill
New home economy by Valerie Barrett, Carol Tennant, Sally Mansfield and
Mitzie Wilson
New recipes and introduction by Linda Doeser
Edited by Fiona Biggs
Nutritional analysis by Fiona Hunter

Notes for the Reader
This book uses both metric and imperial measurements. Follow the same
units of measurement throughout; do not mix metric and imperial. All spoon
measurements are level: teaspoons are assumed to be 5 ml, and tablespoons
are assumed to be 15 ml. Unless otherwise stated, milk is assumed to be full fat,
eggs and individual vegetables are medium, and pepper is freshly ground
black pepper. Unless otherwise stated, all root vegetables should be peeled
prior to using.

Garnishes, decorations and serving suggestions are all optional and not
necessarily included in the recipe ingredients or method. Any optional
ingredients and seasoning to taste are not included in the nutritional analysis.
The times given are an approximate guide only. Preparation times differ
according to the techniques used by different people and the cooking times
may also vary from those given. Optional ingredients, variations or serving
suggestions have not been included in the time calculations.

Vegetarians should be aware that some of the ready-made ingredients used in the
recipes in this book may contain animal products. Always check the packaging
before use.

Contents

Introduction

Pasta's immense popularity is hardly surprising, given that it is astonishingly versatile, easy to cook, nourishing, inexpensive and, in its dried form, keeps for ages. In short, it is arguably the most useful ingredient in the kitchen.

It goes with just about every other foodstuff imaginable to create a range of taste sensations – rich and creamy, light and refreshing, hot and spicy, simple and basic or luxurious and impressive. It may be served hot as a main course or cold as a substantial salad or as part of a picnic, buffet or barbecue and is a delicious and valuable addition to all kinds of soups. It is as tasty partnered with vegetarian ingredients, from tomatoes and mushrooms to cheese and herbs, as it is with all kinds of meat and poultry, fish and seafood.

Pasta is the perfect choice for today's busy lifestyle as there are many dishes that can be prepared and cooked within 30 minutes and some that take only half that time. It's great for midweek family meals, especially as almost all children really love it, and is also ideal for easy, informal entertaining. Whether you're looking for a warming and filling supper to serve on a chilly winter's evening or a delicately flavoured al fresco summer lunch, pasta fits the bill.

Nutritionists recommend that cereals should comprise 33 per cent of a well-balanced diet. Pasta is high in complex carbohydrates, providing a steady release of energy, as well as being an important source of fibre. It contains very little fat. Depending on the type of pasta, it can be a useful source of protein as well as important minerals and vitamins.

Pasta needs a lot of room and a lot of water to cook perfectly, so use a large saucepan.

Pasta is very versatile so it's easy to find fabulous recipes for all occasions and every season of the year.

Double Cheese Macaroni *8*

Tomato, Olive & Mozzarella Pasta Salad *10*

Spinach & Ricotta Cannelloni *12*

Fresh Tomato Soup with Pasta *14*

Penne with Asparagus & Blue Cheese *16*

Pumpkin Ravioli *18*

Chilli Broccoli Pasta *20*

Spaghetti Olio E Aglio *22*

Ziti with Rocket *24*

Spicy Vegetable Lasagne *26*

Pasta with Leek & Butternut Squash *28*

Mushroom Cannelloni *30*

Hearty Bean & Pasta Soup *32*

Pappardelle with Cherry Tomatoes, Rocket & Mozzarella *34*

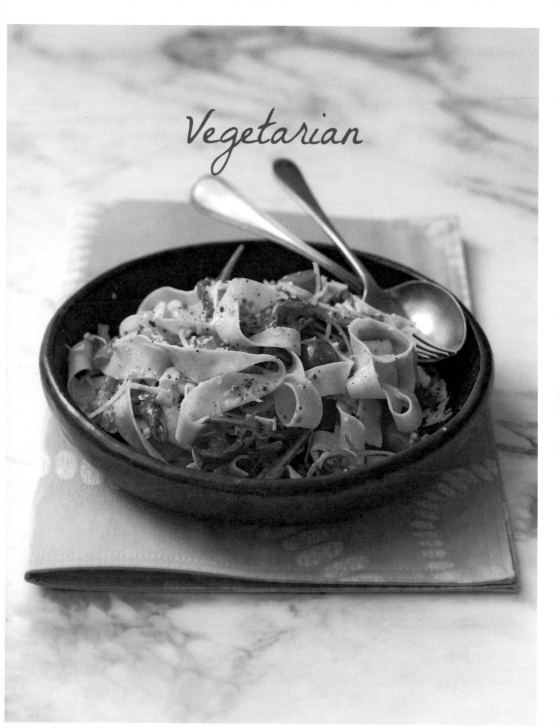

Vegetarian

Double Cheese Macaroni

 SERVES 4

 PREP TIME:
10 minutes

 COOKING TIME:
15 minutes

nutritional information per serving	1109 kcals, 66g fat, 24g sat fat, 9g total sugars, 3g salt

This is an especially rich and tasty variation of a family favourite, equally popular with children and adults.

INGREDIENTS

225 g/8 oz dried macaroni

250 g/9 oz ricotta-style vegetarian cheese

1½ tbsp wholegrain mustard

3 tbsp snipped fresh chives, plus extra to garnish

200 g/7 oz cherry tomatoes, halved

100 g/3½ oz sun-dried tomatoes in oil, drained and chopped

butter or oil, for greasing

100 g/3½ oz vegetarian Cheddar cheese, grated

salt and pepper

1. Preheat the grill to high. Bring a large saucepan of lightly salted water to the boil. Add the pasta, bring back to the boil and cook for 8–10 minutes, until tender but still firm to the bite. Drain.

2. In a large bowl, mix the ricotta-style cheese with the mustard and chives and season to taste with salt and pepper.

3. Stir in the macaroni, cherry tomatoes and sun-dried tomatoes and mix well.

4. Grease a 1.7-litre/3-pint shallow ovenproof dish. Spoon in the macaroni mixture, spreading evenly.

5. Sprinkle the Cheddar cheese over the macaroni mixture and cook under the preheated grill for 4–5 minutes, until golden and bubbling. Serve the macaroni immediately sprinkled with extra chives.

2

3

5

COOK'S NOTE
For a richer dish, tear 125 g/4½ oz mozzarella-style vegetarian cheese into small pieces and stir into the macaroni with the tomatoes.

Tomato, Olive & Mozzarella Pasta Salad

 SERVES 4

 PREP TIME
5 minutes

 COOKING TIME
10 minutes

nutritional information per serving	385 kcals, 36g fat, 10g sat fat, 8g total sugars, 0.7g salt

When you taste this classic combination of ingredients, you'll know why it is so popular in Italy.

INGREDIENTS

225 g/8 oz dried conchiglie

50 g/1¾ oz pine nuts

350 g/12 oz cherry tomatoes, halved

1 red pepper, deseeded and cut into bite-size chunks

1 red onion, chopped

200 g/7 oz vegetarian mozzarella cheese, cut into small pieces

12 black olives, stoned

25 g/1 oz fresh basil leaves

Parmesan-style vegetarian cheese shavings, to garnish

salt

dressing
5 tbsp extra virgin olive oil

2 tbsp balsamic vinegar

1 tbsp chopped fresh basil

salt and pepper

1. Bring a large saucepan of lightly salted water to the boil. Add the pasta, bring back to the boil and cook for 8–10 minutes, until tender but still firm to the bite. Drain thoroughly and leave to cool.

2. Meanwhile, heat a dry frying pan over a low heat, add the pine nuts, and cook, shaking the pan frequently, for 1–2 minutes until lightly toasted. Remove from the heat, transfer to a dish and leave to cool.

3. To make the dressing, put all the ingredients in a small bowl and mix together well. Cover with clingfilm and set aside.

4. Divide the pasta among four serving bowls. Add the pine nuts, tomatoes, pepper, onion, mozzarella cheese and olives to each bowl. Sprinkle over the basil, then drizzle over the dressing. Garnish with Parmesan-style cheese shavings and serve.

Spinach & Ricotta Cannelloni

 SERVES 4 PREP TIME: 20 minutes 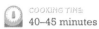 COOKING TIME: 40–45 minutes

nutritional information per serving	591 kcals, 28g fat, 16g sat fat, 9g total sugars, 1.1g salt

Cannelloni started life as sheets of pasta (lasagne), which were rolled around a filling, but now tubes of pasta, ready for stuffing, are available.

INGREDIENTS

melted butter, for greasing

12 dried cannelloni tubes, each about 7.5 cm/3 inches long

salt and pepper

filling

140 g/5 oz frozen spinach, thawed and drained

115 g/4 oz ricotta-style vegetarian cheese

1 egg

3 tbsp grated Parmesan-style vegetarian cheese

pinch of freshly grated nutmeg

cheese sauce

25 g/1 oz butter

2 tbsp plain flour

600 ml/1 pint hot milk

85 g/3 oz vegetarian blue cheese, grated

1. Preheat the oven to 180°C/350°F/Gas Mark 4. Grease a rectangular ovenproof dish with the melted butter.

2. Bring a large saucepan of lightly salted water to the boil. Add the pasta, bring back to the boil and cook for 6–7 minutes, until nearly tender. Drain and rinse, then spread out on a clean tea towel.

3. For the filling, put the spinach and ricotta-style cheese into a food processor or blender and process briefly until combined. Add the egg and Parmesan-style cheese and process to a smooth paste. Transfer to a bowl, add the nutmeg and season to taste with salt and pepper.

4. Spoon the filling into a piping bag fitted with a 1-cm/½-inch nozzle. Carefully open a cannelloni tube and pipe in a little of the filling. Place the filled tube in the prepared dish and repeat.

5. For the cheese sauce, melt the butter in a saucepan. Add the flour to the butter and cook over a low heat, stirring constantly, for 1 minute. Remove from the heat and gradually stir in the hot milk. Return to the heat and bring to the boil, stirring constantly. Simmer over a low heat, stirring frequently, for 10 minutes, until thickened and smooth.

6. Remove from the heat, stir in the vegetarian blue cheese and season to taste with salt and pepper.

7. Spoon the cheese sauce over the filled cannelloni. Cover the dish with foil and bake in the preheated oven for 20–25 minutes. Serve immediately.

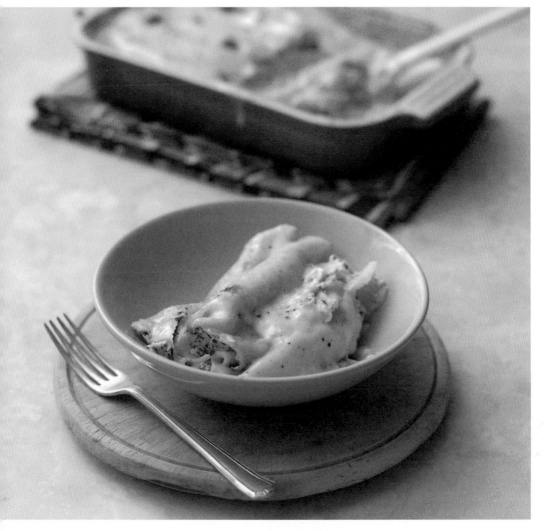

Fresh Tomato Soup with Pasta

 SERVES 4

 PREP TIME: 15 minutes

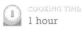 COOKING TIME: 1 hour

nutritional information per serving	135 kcals, 3.5g fat, 0.6g sat fat, 6g total sugars, 0.4g salt

Tomatoes are our major source of dietary lycopene, a carotene antioxidant that fights heart disease and may help prevent prostate cancer. They also contain vitamin C, quercetin and lutein.

INGREDIENTS

1 tbsp olive oil
4 large plum tomatoes
1 onion, cut into quarters
1 garlic clove, thinly sliced
1 celery stick, roughly chopped
500 ml/18 fl oz vegetable stock
55 g/2 oz dried soup pasta
salt and pepper
chopped fresh flat-leaf parsley, to garnish

1. Pour the oil into a large heavy-based saucepan and add the tomatoes, onion, garlic and celery. Cover and cook over a low heat, occasionally shaking gently, for 45 minutes, until pulpy.

2. Transfer the mixture to a food processor or blender and process to a smooth purée.

3. Push the purée through a sieve into a clean saucepan.

4. Add the stock and bring to the boil. Add the pasta, bring back to the boil and cook for 8–10 minutes, until the pasta is tender but still firm to the bite. Season to taste with salt and pepper. Ladle into warmed bowls, garnish with parsley and serve immediately.

1

3

4

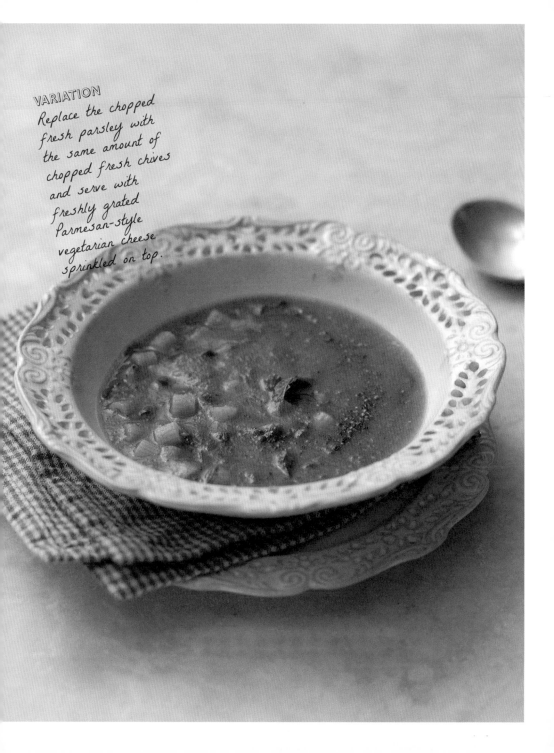

VARIATION
Replace the chopped
fresh parsley with
the same amount of
chopped fresh chives
and serve with
freshly grated
Parmesan-style
vegetarian cheese
sprinkled on top.

Penne with Asparagus & Blue Cheese

 SERVES 4

 PREP TIME:
10 minutes

 COOKING TIME:
15 minutes

nutritional information per serving	805 kcals, 48g fat, 28g sat fat, 5g total sugars, 1.1g salt

It's hard to believe that a dish so stunning is also so simple and requires almost no effort to prepare.

INGREDIENTS

450 g/1 lb asparagus spears

1 tbsp olive oil

225 g/8 oz vegetarian blue cheese, crumbled

175 ml/6 fl oz double cream

350 g/12 oz dried penne

salt and pepper

1. Preheat the oven to 230°C/450°F/Gas Mark 8. Place the asparagus spears in a single layer in a shallow ovenproof dish. Sprinkle with the oil and season to taste with salt and pepper. Turn to coat in the oil and seasoning. Roast in the preheated oven for 10–12 minutes until slightly browned and just tender. Set aside and keep warm.

2. Meanwhile, combine the cheese with the cream in a bowl. Season to taste with salt and pepper.

3. Bring a large saucepan of lightly salted water to the boil. Add the pasta, bring back to the boil and cook for 8–10 minutes, until tender but still firm to the bite. Drain and transfer to a warmed serving dish. Immediately add the asparagus and the cheese mixture. Toss well until the cheese has melted and the pasta is coated with the sauce. Serve immediately.

1

2

3

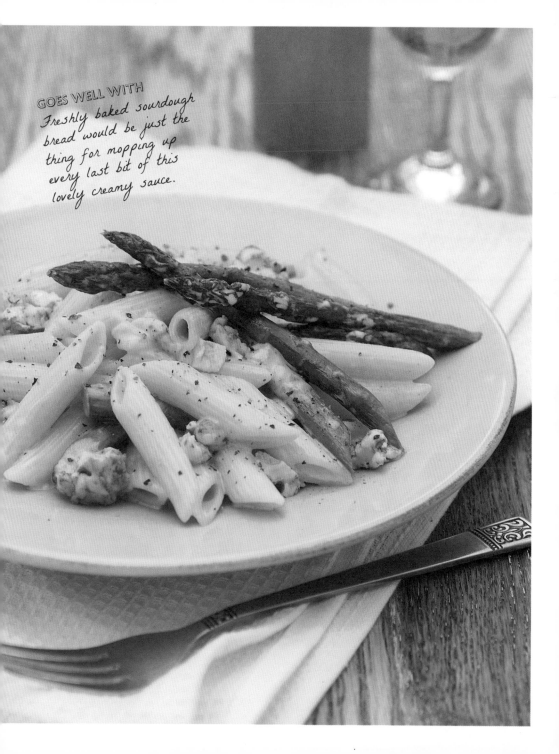

GOES WELL WITH
Freshly baked sourdough
bread would be just the
thing for mopping up
every last bit of this
lovely creamy sauce.

Pumpkin Ravioli

 SERVES 4

PREP TIME:
30 minutes
plus chilling

COOKING TIME:
30-35 minutes

nutritional information per serving	452 kcals, 16g fat, 5g sat fat, 3g total sugars, 0.9g salt

This fabulous filled pasta is a favourite in Emilia-Romagna, a region of northern Italy that is famous for its pasta.

INGREDIENTS

300 g/10½ oz durum wheat flour, plus extra for dusting

2 eggs

1 tbsp oil

½ tsp salt

1 tsp vinegar

3–4 tbsp water

filling

1 tbsp olive oil

450 g/1 lb pumpkin, cubed

1 shallot, finely diced

125 ml/4 fl oz water, plus extra for brushing

55 g/2 oz grated Parmesan-style vegetarian cheese

1 egg

1 tbsp finely chopped fresh parsley

salt and pepper

1. Knead the flour, eggs, oil, salt, vinegar and water into a silky-smooth dough. Wrap the dough in clingfilm and chill in the refrigerator for 1 hour.

2. For the filling, heat the olive oil in a saucepan, add the pumpkin and shallot and sauté for 2–3 minutes, or until the shallot is translucent. Add the water and cook the pumpkin for 15–20 minutes, or until the liquid evaporates. Cool slightly, then mix with the cheese, egg and parsley. Season to taste with salt and pepper.

3. Divide the dough in half. Thinly roll out both pieces on a lightly floured surface. Place small spoonfuls of the pumpkin mixture about 4 cm/1½ inches apart on one sheet of dough. Brush a little water on the spaces in between. Lay the second sheet of dough on top and press down around each piece of filling.

4. Use a pastry wheel to cut out squares and press the edges together with a fork. Leave the ravioli to dry for 30 minutes, then bring a large saucepan of lightly salted water to the boil. Add the ravioli, bring back to the boil and cook over a medium heat for 8–10 minutes, until tender, but still firm to the bite. Remove the ravioli with a slotted spoon and drain well on kitchen paper. Serve immediately.

Chilli Broccoli Pasta

 SERVES 4   PREP TIME: 5 minutes   COOKING TIME: 10–15 minutes

nutritional information per serving	300 kcals, 11g fat, 1.5g sat fat, 3g total sugars, trace salt

A dish made with these ingredients can't fail - they just seem right together. Good for serving to a crowd.

INGREDIENTS

225 g/8 oz dried penne or macaroni

225 g/8 oz head of broccoli, cut into florets

50 ml/2 fl oz extra virgin olive oil

2 large garlic cloves, chopped

2 fresh red chillies, deseeded and diced

8 cherry tomatoes

handful of fresh basil leaves, to garnish

salt

1. Bring a large saucepan of lightly salted water to the boil. Add the pasta, return to the boil and cook for 8–10 minutes, until tender but still firm to the bite. Drain the pasta, refresh under cold running water and drain again. Set aside.

2. Meanwhile bring a separate saucepan of lightly salted water to the boil, add the broccoli and cook for 5 minutes. Drain, refresh under cold running water and drain again.

3. Heat the oil in a large, heavy-based frying pan over high heat. Add the garlic, chillies and tomatoes and cook, stirring constantly, for 1 minute.

4. Add the broccoli and mix well. Cook for 2 minutes, stirring, to heat through. Add the pasta and mix well again. Cook for a further minute. Transfer the pasta to a large, warmed serving bowl and serve immediately, garnished with basil leaves.

2

3

4

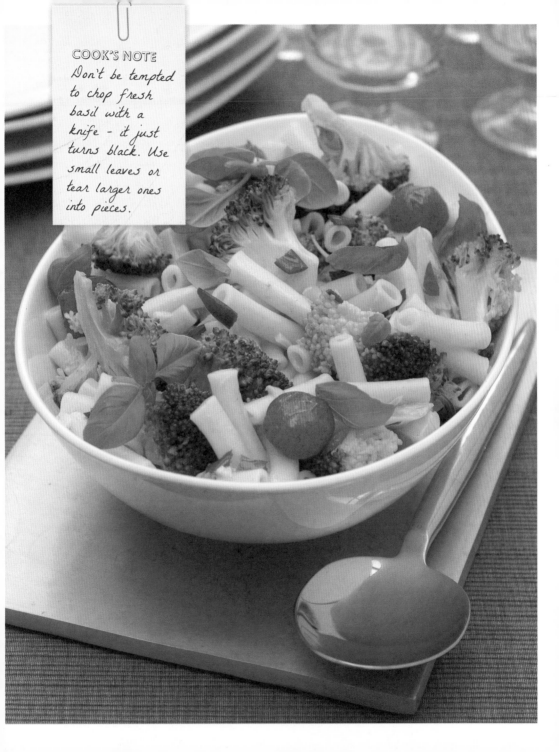

COOK'S NOTE
Don't be tempted to chop fresh basil with a knife - it just turns black. Use small leaves or tear larger ones into pieces.

Spaghetti Olio E Aglio

 SERVES 4

 PREP TIME:
5 minutes

 COOKING TIME:
10 minutes

nutritional information per serving	590 kcals, 25g fat, 3.5g sat fat, 3.5g total sugars, trace salt

An inexpensive dish created by the poor, this Roman classic is now popular throughout Italy.

INGREDIENTS

450 g/1 lb dried spaghetti
125 ml/4 fl oz extra virgin olive oil
3 garlic cloves, finely chopped
3 tbsp chopped fresh flat-leaf parsley
salt and pepper

1. Bring a large saucepan of lightly salted water to the boil. Add the pasta, bring back to the boil and cook for 8–10 minutes, until tender but still firm to the bite.

2. Meanwhile, heat the oil in a heavy-based frying pan. Add the garlic and a pinch of salt and cook over a low heat, stirring constantly, for 3–4 minutes, or until golden. Do not allow the garlic to brown or it will taste bitter. Remove the frying pan from the heat.

3. Drain the pasta and transfer to a warmed serving dish. Pour in the garlic-flavoured oil, then add the chopped parsley and season to taste with salt and pepper. Toss well and serve immediately.

TO SERVE
Cooked pasta gets cold quickly, so make sure to transfer to a warmed serving plate once drained.

Ziti with Rocket

 SERVES 4   PREP TIME: 20 minutes plus resting   COOKING TIME: 15 minutes

nutritional information per serving	435 kcals, 16g fat, 2g sat fat, 2.5g total sugars, trace salt

This pungent dish from Puglia in the 'heel' of Italy looks and tastes absolutely delicious.

INGREDIENTS

2 fresh red chillies, thinly sliced, plus 4 whole chillies to garnish

350 g/12 oz dried ziti, broken into 4-cm/1½-inch lengths

5 tbsp extra virgin olive oil

2 garlic cloves, left whole

200 g/7 oz rocket

Parmesan-style vegetarian cheese, grated

salt

1. For the red chilli garnish, use a sharp knife to remove the tip and cut the chilli lengthways, almost to the stem. Deseed and repeat the cutting process to create 'petals' of an equal length. Place the flowers in a bowl of iced water for 15–20 minutes to encourage the petals to fan out.

2. Bring a large saucepan of lightly salted water to the boil. Add the pasta, bring back to the boil and cook for 8–10 minutes, until tender but still firm to the bite.

3. Meanwhile, heat the oil in a large, heavy-based frying pan. Add the garlic, rocket and sliced chillies and fry for 5 minutes, or until the rocket has wilted.

4. Stir 2 tablespoons of the pasta cooking water into the rocket, then drain the pasta and add to the frying pan. Cook, stirring frequently, for 2 minutes, then transfer to a warmed serving dish. Remove and discard the garlic cloves and sliced chillies, garnish with red chilli flowers and serve immediately with the Parmesan-style cheese.

1

3

4

GOES WELL WITH
This would be good
with plum tomatoes
roasted with garlic,
dressed with olive oil
and balsamic vinegar
and served warm
or cold.

Spicy Vegetable Lasagne

 SERVES 4

 PREP TIME
15 minutes
plus standing time

 COOKING TIME
55 minutes

nutritional information per serving	534 kcals, 28g fat, 12g sat fat, 15g total sugars, 0.8g salt

This colourful and tasty lasagne has layers of diced and sliced vegetables in tomato sauce, all topped with a rich cheese sauce.

INGREDIENTS

1 aubergine, sliced
3 tbsp olive oil
2 garlic cloves, crushed
1 red onion, halved and sliced
3 mixed peppers, deseeded and diced
225 g/8 oz mushrooms, sliced
2 celery sticks, sliced
1 courgette, diced
½ tsp chilli powder
½ tsp ground cumin
2 tomatoes, chopped
300 ml/10 fl oz passata
3 tbsp chopped fresh basil
8 dried no pre-cook lasagne sheets
salt and pepper

cheese sauce
2 tbsp butter
1 tbsp flour
150 ml/5 fl oz vegetable stock
300 ml/10 fl oz milk
75 g/2¾ oz vegetarian Cheddar cheese, grated
1 tsp Dijon mustard
1 egg, beaten

1. Place the aubergine slices in a colander, sprinkle with salt and leave for 20 minutes. Rinse under cold water, drain and reserve.

2. Preheat the oven to 180°C/350°F/Gas Mark 4. Heat the oil in a saucepan. Add the garlic and onion and sauté for 1–2 minutes. Add the peppers, mushrooms, celery and courgette and cook, stirring constantly, for 3–4 minutes.

3. Stir in the chilli powder and cumin and cook for 1 minute. Mix in the tomatoes, passata and 2 tablespoons of the basil and season to taste with salt and pepper.

4. For the sauce, melt the butter in a saucepan. Stir in the flour and cook for 1 minute. Remove from the heat, gradually stir in the stock and milk, return to the heat, then add half the cheese and all the mustard. Boil, stirring, until thickened. Stir in the remaining basil. Remove from the heat and stir in the egg.

5. Place half the lasagne sheets in an ovenproof dish. Top with half the vegetable and tomato sauce, then half the aubergines. Repeat and then spoon the cheese sauce on top. Sprinkle with the remaining cheese and bake in the preheated oven for 40 minutes, until golden and bubbling. Serve immediately.

Pasta with Leek & Butternut Squash

 SERVES 4   PREP TIME: 15 minutes   COOKING TIME: 30 minutes

nutritional information per serving	334 kcals, 5g fat, 1.5g sat fat, 9g total sugars, 0.4g salt

This unusual dish combines the sweetness of roasted vegetables with warm spice and aromatic coriander.

INGREDIENTS

150 g/5½ oz baby leeks, cut into 2-cm/¾-inch slices

175 g/6 oz butternut squash, deseeded and cut into 2-cm/¾-inch chunks

1½ tbsp medium curry paste

1 tsp vegetable oil

175 g/6 oz cherry tomatoes

250 g/9 oz dried farfalle

2 tbsp chopped fresh coriander

salt

white sauce

250 ml/9 fl oz skimmed milk

20 g/¾ oz cornflour

1 tsp mustard powder

1 small onion, left whole

2 small bay leaves

4 tsp grated Parmesan-style vegetarian cheese

1. To make the white sauce, put the milk into a saucepan with the cornflour, mustard powder, onion and bay leaves. Whisk over a medium heat until thick. Remove from the heat, discard the onion and bay leaves and stir in the cheese. Set aside, stirring occasionally to prevent a skin forming. Preheat the oven to 200°C/400°F/Gas Mark 6.

2. Bring a large saucepan of water to the boil, add the leeks and cook for 2 minutes. Add the butternut squash and cook for a further 2 minutes. Drain in a colander. Mix the curry paste with the oil in a large bowl. Toss the leeks and butternut squash in the mixture to coat thoroughly.

3. Transfer the leeks and squash to a non-stick baking sheet and roast in the preheated oven for 10 minutes until golden brown. Add the tomatoes and roast for a further 5 minutes.

4. Meanwhile, bring a large saucepan of lightly salted water to the boil. Add the pasta, bring back to the boil and cook for 8–10 minutes, until tender but still firm to the bite. Drain well. Put the white sauce into a large saucepan and warm over a low heat. Add the leeks, squash, tomatoes and coriander and stir in the pasta. Transfer to warmed plates and serve immediately.

Mushroom Cannelloni

 SERVES 4   PREP TIME: 15 minutes   COOKING TIME: 50 minutes

nutritional information per serving	866 kcals, 51g fat, 16g sat fat, 13g total sugars, 1.5g salt

This dish is perfect for real mushroom-lovers. You can use any combination of wild mushrooms you wish. Porcini especially add an extra strong and nutty flavour.

INGREDIENTS

12 dried cannelloni tubes

6 tbsp olive oil, plus extra for brushing

1 onion, finely chopped

2 garlic cloves, finely chopped

800 g/1 lb 12 oz canned chopped tomatoes

1 tbsp tomato purée

8 black olives, stoned and chopped

25 g/1 oz butter

450 g/1 lb wild mushrooms, finely chopped

85 g/3 oz fresh breadcrumbs

150 ml/5 fl oz milk

225 g/8 oz vegetarian-style ricotta cheese

6 tbsp freshly-grated Parmesan-style vegetarian cheese

2 tbsp pine nuts

2 tbsp flaked almonds

salt and pepper

1. Preheat the oven to 190°C/375°F/Gas Mark 5. Bring a large saucepan of lightly salted water to the boil. Add the cannelloni tubes, return to the boil and cook for 8–10 minutes, or until tender but still firm to the bite. With a slotted spoon, transfer the cannelloni tubes to a plate and pat dry. Brush a large ovenproof dish with oil.

2. Heat 2 tablespoons of the oil in a frying pan, add the onion and half the garlic and cook over a low heat for 5 minutes, or until softened. Add the tomatoes and their can juices, tomato purée and olives and season to taste with salt and pepper. Bring to the boil and cook for 3–4 minutes. Pour the sauce into the ovenproof dish.

3. To make the filling, melt the butter in a heavy-based frying pan. Add the mushrooms and remaining garlic and cook over a medium heat, stirring frequently, for 3–5 minutes, or until tender.

4. Remove the frying pan from the heat. Mix the breadcrumbs, milk and remaining oil together in a large bowl, then stir in the ricotta-style cheese, the mushroom mixture and 4 tablespoons of the Parmesan-style cheese. Season to taste with salt and pepper.

5. Fill the cannelloni tubes with the mushroom mixture and place them in the prepared dish. Brush with oil and sprinkle with the remaining Parmesan-style cheese, the pine nuts and almonds. Bake in the preheated oven for 25 minutes until golden and bubbling. Serve immediately.

Hearty Bean & Pasta Soup

 SERVES 4

 PREP TIME
10 minutes

 COOKING TIME
40 minutes

nutritional information per serving	456 kcals, 16g fat, 4g sat fat, 8g total sugars, 1.3g salt

Add a little Tuscan sunshine to your dinner table with this colourful and satisfying traditional soup.

INGREDIENTS

4 tbsp olive oil

1 onion, finely chopped

1 celery stick, finely chopped

1 carrot, diced

1 bay leaf

1.2 litres/2 pints vegetable stock

400 g/14 oz canned chopped tomatoes

175 g/6 oz dried farfalle

400 g/14 oz canned cannellini beans, drained and rinsed

200 g/7 oz spinach or chard, thick stalks removed and shredded

salt and pepper

40 g/1½ oz Parmesan-style vegetarian cheese, finely grated, to serve

1. Heat the oil in a large, heavy-based saucepan. Add the onion, celery and carrot and cook over a medium heat for 10 minutes, stirring occasionally, until the vegetables slightly soften. Add the bay leaf, stock and tomatoes, then bring to the boil.

2. Reduce the heat, cover and simmer for 15 minutes, or until the vegetables are just tender. Add the pasta and beans, bring back to the boil and cook for 8–10 minutes, until the pasta is tender but still firm to the bite.

3. Stir occasionally to prevent the pasta sticking to the bottom of the pan and burning. Season to taste with salt and pepper, add the spinach and cook for a further 2 minutes, or until tender. Remove and discard the bay leaf. Ladle the soup into warmed bowls and serve immediately with grated Parmesan-style cheese.

Pappardelle with Cherry Tomatoes, Rocket & Mozzarella

 SERVES 4   PREP TIME: 5 minutes   COOKING TIME: 15 minutes

nutritional information per serving	1218 kcals, 46g fat, 23g sat, 10g total sugars, 1.6g salt

Creamy cheese, pungent leaves and sweet tomatoes are a great combination that tastes as good as it looks.

INGREDIENTS

400 g/14 oz dried pappardelle

2 tbsp olive oil

1 garlic clove, chopped

350 g/12 oz cherry tomatoes, halved

85 g/3 oz rocket leaves

300 g/10½ oz vegetarian mozzarella cheese, chopped

salt and pepper

grated Parmesan-style vegetarian cheese, to serve

1. Bring a large saucepan of lightly salted water to the boil. Add the pasta, bring back to the boil and cook for 8–10 minutes, until tender but still firm to the bite.

2. Meanwhile, heat the oil in a frying pan over a medium heat and fry the garlic, stirring, for 1 minute, without browning.

3. Add the tomatoes, season well with salt and pepper and cook gently for 2–3 minutes, until softened.

4. Drain the pasta and stir into the frying pan. Add the rocket leaves and mozzarella cheese, then stir until the leaves wilt.

5. Serve the pasta in warmed dishes, sprinkled with the Parmesan-style vegetarian cheese.

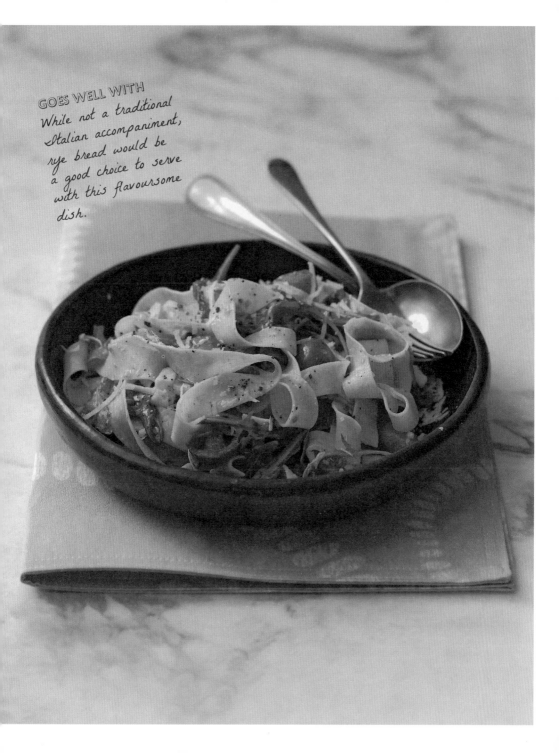

GOES WELL WITH
While not a traditional
Italian accompaniment,
rye bread would be
a good choice to serve
with this flavoursome
dish.

Spaghetti Bolognese *38*

Turkey Pasta Bake *40*

Lasagne al Forno *42*

Farfalle with Chicken & Broccoli *44*

Spicy Chicken Pasta *46*

Pepperoni Pasta *48*

Spaghetti & Corned Beef *50*

Beef Burger Pasta *52*

Spaghetti with Bacon & Crispy Breadcrumbs *54*

Pasta with Harissa Turkey Meatballs *56*

Penne Pasta with Sausage *58*

Spaghetti Carbonara *60*

Pasta with Bacon & Tomatoes *62*

Chicken with Creamy Penne *64*

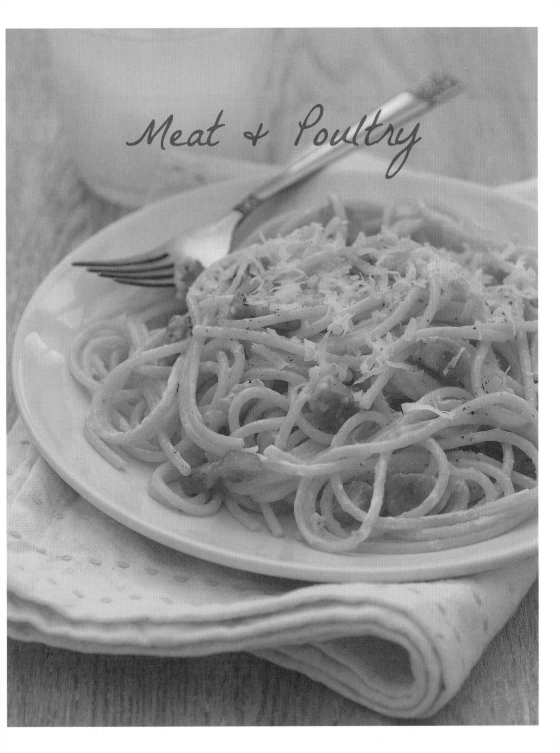

Meat & Poultry

Spaghetti Bolognese

 SERVES 4   PREP TIME: 15 minutes   COOKING TIME: 40 minutes

nutritional information per serving	535 kcals, 14g fat, 4g sat fat, 5g total sugars, 0.4g salt

This classic meat sauce (ragù) from Bologna can also be made with minced veal or half beef and half pork.

INGREDIENTS

350 g/12 oz spaghetti or pasta of your choice

fresh Parmesan cheese shavings, to garnish (optional)

sprigs of thyme, to garnish

crusty bread, to serve

bolognese sauce
2 tbsp olive oil

1 onion, finely chopped

2 garlic cloves, finely chopped

1 carrot, peeled and finely chopped

85 g/3 oz mushrooms, peeled and sliced or chopped (optional)

1 tsp dried oregano

½ tsp dried thyme

1 bay leaf

280 g/10 oz lean beef mince

300 ml/10 fl oz stock

300 ml/10 fl oz passata

salt and pepper

1. To make the sauce, heat the oil in a heavy-based, non-stick saucepan. Add the onion and sauté, half covered, for 5 minutes, or until soft. Add the garlic, carrot and mushrooms, if using, and sauté for a further 3 minutes, stirring occasionally.

2. Add the herbs and mince to the pan and cook until the meat has browned, stirring regularly.

3. Add the stock and passata. Reduce the heat, season to taste with salt and pepper and cook over a medium–low heat, half covered, for 15–20 minutes, or until the sauce has reduced and thickened. Remove the bay leaf.

4. Meanwhile, bring a large saucepan of lightly salted water to the boil. Add the pasta, bring back to the boil and cook for 8–10 minutes, until tender but still firm to the bite. Drain well and mix together the pasta and sauce until the pasta is well coated. Serve immediately with crusty bread and garnished with Parmesan cheese shavings, if using, and sprigs of thyme.

Turkey Pasta Bake

 SERVES 6

 PREP TIME:
15 minutes

 COOKING TIME:
50 minutes

nutritional information
per serving | 614 kcals, 27g fat, 15g sat fat, 8g total sugars, 1.1g salt

*This fail-safe bake is filling, incredibly easy to make
and economical – perfect for a midweek family supper.*

INGREDIENTS

100 g/3½ oz butter
1 tbsp olive oil
1 onion, finely chopped
450 g/1 lb fresh turkey mince
2 tbsp plain flour
700 ml/1¼ pints milk
1 tsp Dijon mustard
85 g/3 oz Cheddar cheese, grated
280 g/10 oz dried macaroni
2 tbsp chopped fresh parsley
85 g/3 oz fresh breadcrumbs
salt

1. Melt 25 g/1 oz of the butter with the oil in a frying pan. Add the onion and cook over a low heat, stirring occasionally, for 5 minutes until soft. Add the turkey, increase the heat to medium and cook, stirring frequently, for 7–8 minutes, until evenly browned. Remove the pan from the heat, transfer the turkey and onion to a bowl with a slotted spoon and set aside.

2. Melt 40 g/1½ oz of the remaining butter in a saucepan, stir in the flour and cook, stirring constantly, for 1 minute. Remove the pan from the heat and gradually whisk in the milk, then return to the heat and bring to the boil, whisking constantly until thickened. Remove the pan from the heat and stir in the mustard, turkey mixture and 55 g/2 oz of the cheese.

3. Preheat the oven to 180°C/350°F/Gas Mark 4. Bring a large saucepan of lightly salted water to the boil. Add the pasta, bring back to the boil and cook for 8–10 minutes, until tender but still firm to the bite. Drain and stir into the turkey mixture with the parsley.

4. Spoon the mixture into an ovenproof dish, sprinkle with the breadcrumbs and remaining cheese and dot with the remaining butter. Bake in the preheated oven for 25 minutes until golden and bubbling. Serve immediately.

Lasagne al Forno

 SERVES 6   PREP TIME: 15 minutes   COOKING TIME: 2¼ hours

nutritional information per serving | 629 kcals, 71g fat, 30g sat fat, 5g total sugars, 2.8g salt

You need plenty of time to make a baked lasagne with an authentic flavour, but it is worth it.

INGREDIENTS

175 ml/6 fl oz olive oil

55 g/2 oz butter

100 g/3½ oz pancetta

1 onion, finely chopped

1 celery stick, finely chopped

1 carrot, finely chopped

350 g/12 oz braising steak, in a single piece

5 tbsp red wine

2 tbsp sun-dried tomato purée

200 g/7 oz Italian sausage

2 eggs

150 g/5½ oz freshly grated Parmesan cheese

30 g/1 oz fresh breadcrumbs

350 g/12 oz ricotta cheese

8 dried no pre-cook lasagne sheets

350 g/12 oz mozzarella cheese, sliced

salt and pepper

chopped fresh parsley, to garnish

1. Heat 125 ml/4 fl oz of the oil with the butter in a large saucepan. Add the pancetta, onion, celery and carrot and cook over a low heat, until soft. Increase the heat to medium, add the steak and cook until evenly browned. Stir in the wine and tomato purée, season with salt and pepper and bring to the boil. Reduce the heat, cover and simmer gently for 1½ hours, until the steak is tender.

2. Meanwhile, heat 2 tablespoons of the remaining oil in a frying pan. Add the sausage and cook for 8–10 minutes. Remove from the pan and discard the skin. Thinly slice the sausage and set aside. Transfer the steak to a chopping board and finely dice. Return half the steak to the sauce.

3. Mix the remaining steak in a bowl with 1 egg, 1 tablespoon of the Parmesan cheese and the breadcrumbs. Shape into walnut-sized balls. Heat the remaining oil in a frying pan, add the meatballs and cook for 5–8 minutes, until brown. Pass the ricotta through a sieve into a bowl. Stir in the remaining egg and 4 tablespoons of the remaining Parmesan cheese.

4. Preheat the oven to 180°C/350°F/Gas Mark 4. In a rectangular ovenproof dish, make layers with the lasagne sheets, ricotta mixture, meat sauce, meatballs, sausage and mozzarella cheese. Finish with a layer of the ricotta mixture and sprinkle with the remaining Parmesan cheese.

5. Bake the lasagne in the preheated oven for 20–25 minutes, until golden and bubbling. Serve immediately, garnished with chopped parsley.

Farfalle with Chicken & Broccoli

 SERVES 4

 PREP TIME:
10 minutes

 COOKING TIME:
20–25 minutes

nutritional information per serving	707 kcals, 33g fat, 12g sat fat, 3g total sugars, 0.7g salt

This is one of those dishes that looks almost too pretty to eat but it's far too tasty to resist.

INGREDIENTS

4 tbsp olive oil

5 tbsp butter

3 garlic cloves, very finely chopped

450 g/1 lb skinless, boneless chicken breasts, diced

¼ tsp dried chilli flakes

450 g/1 lb small broccoli florets

300 g/10½ oz dried farfalle

175 g/6 oz bottled roasted red peppers, drained and diced

250 ml/9 fl oz chicken stock

salt and pepper

1. Bring a large saucepan of lightly salted water to the boil. Meanwhile, heat the oil and butter in a large frying pan over a medium–low heat and cook the garlic until just beginning to colour.

2. Add the diced chicken, increase the heat to medium and cook for 4–5 minutes, until the chicken is cooked through. Add the chilli flakes and season to taste with salt and pepper. Remove from the heat.

3. Plunge the broccoli into the boiling water and cook for 2 minutes. Remove with a slotted spoon and set aside. Bring the water back to the boil. Add the pasta and cook for 8–10 minutes, until tender but still firm to the bite. Drain thoroughly and add to the chicken mixture in the frying pan. Add the broccoli and roasted peppers. Pour in the stock. Simmer briskly over a medium–high heat, stirring frequently, until most of the liquid has been absorbed.

4. Transfer to warmed dishes and serve immediately.

1

2

3

GOES WELL WITH
The perfect accompaniment would be a light rosé wine or, if you prefer a non-alcoholic drink, sparkling grape or apple juice.

Spicy Chicken Pasta

 SERVES 6

 PREP TIME:
25 minutes
plus marinating

 COOKING TIME:
40 minutes

nutritional information per serving	500 kcals, 11g fat, 2g sat fat, 8g total sugars, 0.4g salt

You have to allow time for the chicken to marinate but this mouth-watering spicy dish is worth the wait.

INGREDIENTS

12 skinless boneless chicken thighs, cubed

1 tbsp groundnut oil

1 red pepper, deseeded and chopped

1 green pepper, deseeded and chopped

200 g/7 oz canned chopped tomatoes

450 g/1 lb dried spaghetti

salt

marinade

2 tbsp finely chopped spring onions, plus extra to garnish

1–2 chillies, deseeded (optional) and chopped

2 garlic cloves, finely chopped

1 tsp ground cinnamon

1 tsp ground allspice

pinch of grated nutmeg

2 tsp soft light brown sugar

2 tbsp groundnut oil

1 tbsp lime juice

1 tbsp white wine vinegar

salt and pepper

1. Put the chicken into a large, non-metallic dish. Mix all the marinade ingredients in a bowl, mashing everything together. Spoon the mixture over the chicken and rub it in with your hands. Cover the dish with clingfilm and leave to marinate in the refrigerator for at least 2 hours, preferably overnight.

2. Heat the oil in a saucepan, add the red pepper and green pepper and cook over a medium–low heat, stirring occasionally, for 5 minutes. Add the chicken and any remaining marinade and cook, stirring frequently, for 5 minutes until cooked through. Add the tomatoes, reduce the heat, cover and simmer, stirring occasionally, for 30 minutes. Check occasionally that the mixture is not drying out – if it is, add a little water.

3. Halfway through the chicken cooking time, bring a large saucepan of lightly salted water to the boil. Add the pasta, bring back to the boil and cook for 8–10 minutes, until tender but still firm to the bite.

4. Drain the pasta, tip it into the pan with the chicken and toss lightly. Transfer to warmed plates, garnish with the spring onion and serve immediately.

Pepperoni Pasta

 SERVES 4 PREP TIME: 10 minutes COOKING TIME: 20 minutes

nutritional information per serving	780 kcals, 33g fat, 10g sat fat, 14g total sugars, 2.8g salt

A sure-fire favourite, this colourful and utterly scrumptious dish will cheer up even the dreariest day.

INGREDIENTS

3 tbsp olive oil

1 onion, chopped

1 red pepper, deseeded and diced

1 orange pepper, deseeded and diced

800 g/1 lb 12 oz canned chopped tomatoes

1 tbsp sun-dried tomato puree

1 tsp paprika

225 g/8 oz pepperoni sausage, sliced

2 tbsp chopped fresh flat-leaf parsley, plus extra to garnish

450 g/1 lb dried penne

salt and pepper

1. Heat 2 tablespoons of the oil in a large heavy-based frying pan. Add the onion and cook over a low heat, stirring occasionally, for 5 minutes, or until softened. Add the red pepper and orange pepper, tomatoes and their can juices, sun-dried tomato puree and paprika and bring to the boil.

2. Add the pepperoni and parsley and season to taste with salt and pepper. Stir well, bring to the boil, then reduce the heat and simmer for 10–15 minutes.

3. Meanwhile, bring a large saucepan of lightly salted water to the boil. Add the pasta, bring back to the boil and cook for 8–10 minutes, until tender but still firm to the bite. Drain well and transfer to a warmed serving dish. Add the remaining olive oil and toss. Add the sauce and toss again. Sprinkle with parsley and serve immediately.

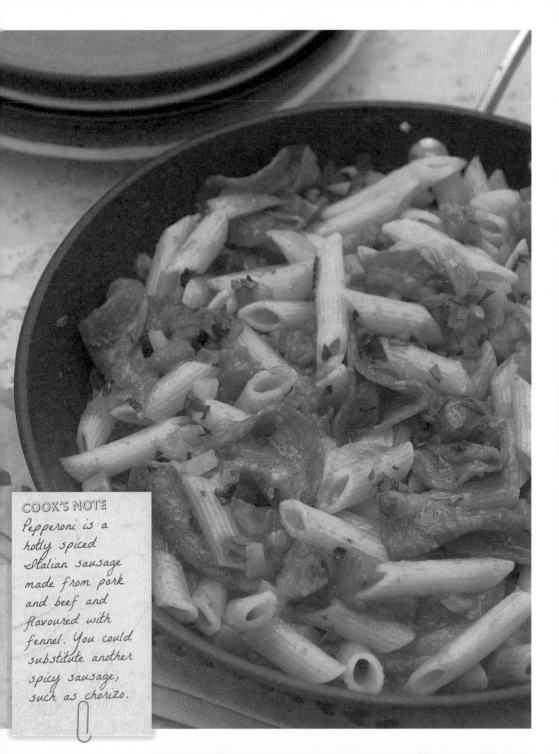

Spaghetti & Corned Beef

 SERVES 4   PREP TIME: 10 minutes   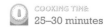 COOKING TIME: 25–30 minutes

nutritional information per serving	742 kcals, 21g fat, 8g sat fat, 8g total sugars, 2.8g salt

Popular with children and extremely economical, this variation of corned beef hash is an easy way to ring the changes in the family menu.

INGREDIENTS

2 tbsp sunflower oil

1 large onion, chopped

2–3 garlic cloves, finely chopped

500 g/1 lb 2 oz corned beef, chopped

400 g/14 oz canned tomatoes

450 g/1 lb dried spaghetti

2 tbsp chopped fresh parsley

pinch of crushed chillies or dash of Tabasco sauce or Worcestershire sauce

salt and pepper

1. Heat the oil in a large frying pan, add the onion and garlic and cook over a medium heat for 5 minutes until just beginning to colour.

2. Add the corned beef and cook, stirring and mashing with a wooden spoon, for 5–8 minutes until it is quite dry. Drain the tomatoes, reserving the can juices, and stir them into the pan. Cook for a further 10 minutes, adding a little of the reserved can juices if the mixture seems to be drying out too much.

3. Meanwhile, bring a large saucepan of lightly salted water to the boil. Add the pasta, bring back to the boil and cook for 8–10 minutes, until tender but still firm to the bite.

4. Drain the pasta and add it to the frying pan. Stir in the parsley and chillies and season to taste with salt and pepper, bearing in mind that corned beef is often quite salty already. Mix well and heat through for a further few minutes. Serve immediately.

Beef Burger Pasta

 SERVES 4   PREP TIME: 10 minutes   COOKING TIME: 20 minutes

nutritional information
per serving   686 kcals, 34g fat, 12g sat fat, 8g total sugars, 0.9g salt

This is a good way to use up leftover burgers, combining them with larder ingredients for a quick and easy meal.

INGREDIENTS

300 g/10½ oz dried conchiglie

350 g/12 oz beef burgers

400 g/14 oz frozen mixed vegetables, such as broccoli, carrots and sweetcorn

400 g/14 oz canned tomatoes, drained

1 garlic clove, finely chopped

1–1½ pickled jalapeño chillies, finely chopped

3 tbsp olive oil

2 tbsp freshly grated Parmesan cheese

salt and pepper

1. Bring a large saucepan of lightly salted water to the boil. Add the pasta, bring back to the boil and cook for 8–10 minutes, until tender but still firm to the bite. Preheat the grill to hot.

2. Meanwhile, cook the burgers under the preheated grill for 7–8 minutes on each side until cooked through. Bring a separate saucepan of lightly salted water to the boil, add the frozen vegetables and cook for about 5 minutes.

3. Drain the vegetables, transfer to a food processor and process briefly until chopped, then tip into a saucepan. Transfer the cooked burgers to the food processor and process briefly until chopped, then add to the pan of vegetables. Stir in the tomatoes, garlic, chillies and oil, season to taste with salt and pepper and reheat gently.

4. Drain the pasta and tip it into a warmed serving bowl. Add the burger and vegetable mixture and toss lightly. Sprinkle with the cheese and serve immediately.

3

3

3

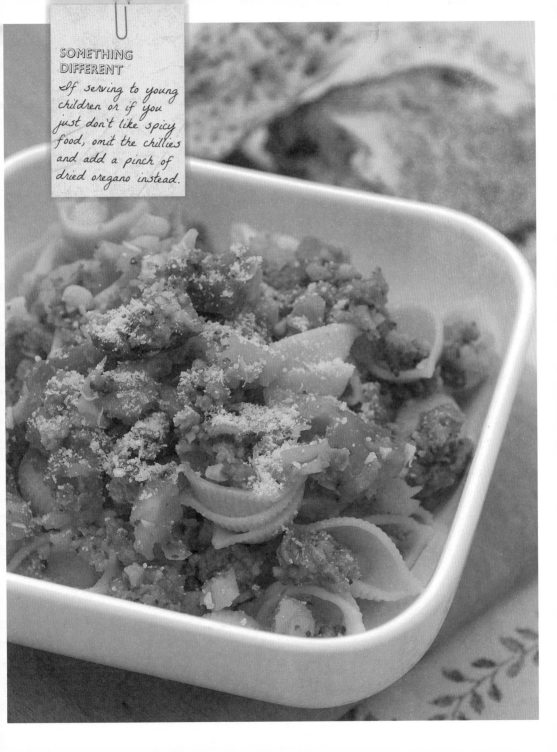

Spaghetti with Bacon & Crispy Breadcrumbs

 SERVES 2   PREP TIME: 10 minutes   COOKING TIME: 10 minutes

nutritional information per serving	787 kcals, 42g fat, 11g sat fat, 4g total sugars, 2.7g salt

Quick, easy and economical, yet truly mouth-watering, this is the perfect midweek family supper.

INGREDIENTS

55 g/2 oz day-old ciabatta bread (approximately one roll)

sprig of fresh rosemary

175 g/6 oz dried spaghetti

2 tsp olive oil

140 g/5 oz smoked streaky bacon, chopped

15 g/½ oz butter

40 g/1½ oz pine nuts

2 garlic cloves, crushed

2–3 tbsp chopped fresh flat-leaf parsley

salt and pepper

1. Put the day-old bread, including any crusts, in a food processor or blender and process until the mixture resembles coarse breadcrumbs. Bruise the rosemary sprig in a pestle and mortar or using a rolling pin to release the flavour.

2. Bring a large saucepan of lightly salted water to the boil. Add the pasta, bring back to the boil and cook for 8–10 minutes, until tender but still firm to the bite.

3. Meanwhile, heat the oil in a large frying pan, add the bacon and rosemary and fry for 2–3 minutes until the bacon is golden brown. Transfer to a warmed serving bowl using a slotted spoon.

4. Add the butter to the bacon fat remaining in the pan. When melted and foaming, add the breadcrumbs, pine nuts and garlic. Fry for 2–3 minutes, stirring until golden brown, then tip into the bowl with the bacon.

5. Drain the pasta and transfer to the bowl with the bacon and breadcrumbs. Add the parsley, season with pepper and toss well. Serve immediately.

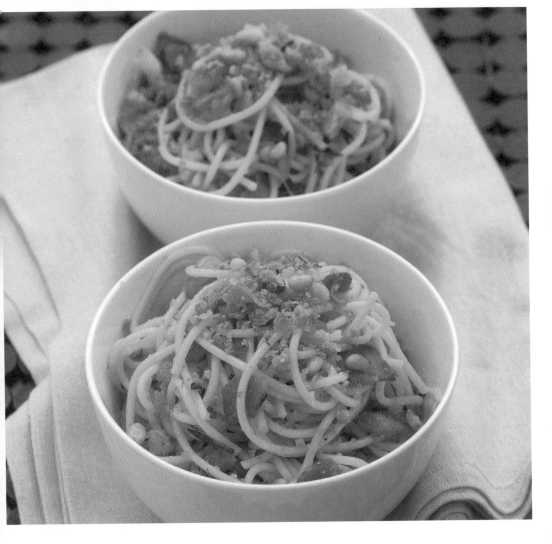

Pasta with Harissa Turkey Meatballs

 SERVES 4

 PREP TIME: 15 minutes

 COOKING TIME: 15–20 minutes

nutritional information per serving	560 kcals, 10g fat, 3g sat fat, 7.5g total sugars, 0.7g salt

If you like spicy food, this North African-style dish is the perfect choice, and you can easily adjust the heat to suit you.

INGREDIENTS

350 g/12 oz fresh turkey mince

55 g/2 oz dry breadcrumbs

6 tbsp Greek-style yogurt

1 egg

½ tsp ground coriander

½ tsp ground cumin

½–1 tsp harissa

3 tbsp finely chopped parsley

350 g/12 oz dried spaghetti or tagliatelle

olive oil, for drizzling

salt and pepper

sauce

400 g/14 oz canned chopped tomatoes

1 small chilli, deseeded and finely chopped

¼ tsp ground cinnamon

½ tsp ground cumin

1. Preheat the oven to 200°C/400°F/Gas Mark 6. Line a baking sheet with baking paper.

2. Mix together the turkey, breadcrumbs, yogurt, egg, coriander, cumin, harissa and parsley in a bowl until thoroughly combined. Season to taste with salt and pepper. Shape the mixture into meatballs about the size of a golf ball and put them on the prepared baking sheet. Bake for 15 minutes until lightly browned.

3. Meanwhile, bring a large saucepan of lightly salted water to the boil. Add the pasta, bring back to the boil and cook for 8–10 minutes, until tender but still firm to the bite. Drain, transfer to a warmed dish, drizzle with oil and toss to coat.

4. Meanwhile, put all the sauce ingredients into a saucepan and simmer, stirring occasionally, for 5 minutes until thickened.

5. Remove the meatballs from the oven and add to the pasta. Pour the sauce over them and toss together. Serve immediately.

Penne Pasta with Sausage

 SERVES 6   PREP TIME: 15 minutes   COOKING TIME: 20–25 minutes

nutritional information per serving	437 kcals, 19g fat, 6g sat fat, 5g total sugars, 1.5g salt

Packed with flavour and lively rather than fiery, this is an ideal dish for informal entertaining.

INGREDIENTS

2 tbsp olive oil

1 red onion, roughly chopped

2 garlic cloves, roughly chopped

6 Italian sausages, skinned and the meat crumbled

½ tsp dried chilli flakes

2 tbsp chopped fresh oregano

400 g/14 oz canned chopped tomatoes

350 g/12 oz dried penne

salt and pepper

1. Heat the oil in a large saucepan, add the onion and cook over a medium heat, stirring frequently, for 6–8 minutes until starting to brown. Add the garlic and the crumbled sausages and cook for 8–10 minutes, breaking up the sausages with a wooden spoon.

2. Add the chilli flakes and oregano and stir well. Pour in the tomatoes and bring to the boil. Place over a low heat and simmer for 4–5 minutes until reduced and thickened. Season to taste with salt and pepper.

3. Meanwhile, bring a large saucepan of lightly salted water to the boil. Add the pasta, bring back to the boil and cook for 8–10 minutes, until tender but still firm to the bite. Drain thoroughly and return to the pan.

4. Pour the sauce into the pasta and stir well. Transfer to warmed serving plates and serve immediately.

Spaghetti Carbonara

 SERVES 4   PREP TIME: 10 minutes   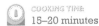 COOKING TIME: 15–20 minutes

nutritional information per serving	1498 kcals, 73g fat, 35g sat fat, 7g total sugars, 4g salt

This popular Italian dish combines pancetta and double cream with two hard cheeses – Parmesan and pecorino.

INGREDIENTS

400 g/14 oz dried spaghetti

4 eggs

4 tbsp double cream

55 g/2 oz grated Parmesan cheese, plus extra to garnish

55 g/2 oz grated pecorino cheese

1 tbsp butter

150 g/5½ oz pancetta, finely diced

salt and pepper

1. Bring a large saucepan of lightly salted water to the boil. Add the pasta, bring back to the boil and cook for 8–10 minutes, until tender but still firm to the bite.

2. Meanwhile, stir together the eggs, cream, Parmesan cheese and pecorino cheese in a bowl. Season to taste with salt and pepper.

3. Melt the butter in a large saucepan, add the pancetta, and fry over a medium heat for 8–10 minutes, until crispy. Drain the spaghetti and add it to the pan while still dripping wet. Pour the cheese sauce over it. Remove the pan from the heat. Toss the spaghetti in the sauce until the eggs begin to thicken but are still creamy.

4. Transfer to warmed plates and serve immediately, sprinkled with pepper and a little more Parmesan cheese.

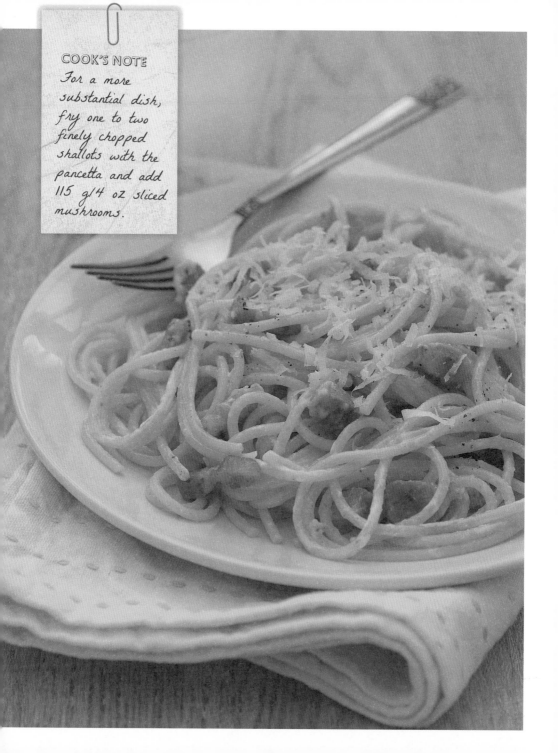

COOK'S NOTE

For a more substantial dish, fry one to two finely chopped shallots with the pancetta and add 115 g/4 oz sliced mushrooms.

Pasta with Bacon & Tomatoes

 SERVES 4

 PREP TIME:
15 minutes

 COOKING TIME:
25–30 minutes

nutritional information per serving	592 kcals, 17g fat, 8g sat fat, 10g total sugars, 1.5g salt

This is an ideal dish to serve in the summer when tomatoes are at their sweetest.

INGREDIENTS

900 g/2 lb small, sweet tomatoes
6 rashers rindless smoked bacon
55 g/2 oz butter
1 onion, chopped
1 garlic clove, crushed
4 fresh oregano sprigs, finely chopped
450 g/1 lb dried orecchiette
salt and pepper
freshly grated pecorino cheese, to serve

1. Blanch the tomatoes in boiling water. Drain, peel and deseed the tomatoes, then roughly chop the flesh.

2. Using a sharp knife, chop the bacon into small dice. Melt the butter in a saucepan. Add the bacon and cook for 2–3 minutes until golden brown.

3. Add the onion and garlic and cook over a medium heat for 5–7 minutes, until just softened.

4. Add the tomatoes and oregano to the pan and then season to taste with salt and pepper. Lower the heat and simmer for 10–12 minutes.

5. Meanwhile, bring a large saucepan of lightly salted water to the boil. Add the pasta, bring back to the boil and cook for 8–10 minutes, until tender but still firm to the bite. Drain the pasta and transfer to a warmed serving bowl. Spoon the bacon and tomato sauce over the pasta, toss to coat and serve immediately with the pecorino cheese.

1

4

5

Chicken with Creamy Penne

 SERVES 2　　 PREP TIME: 5 minutes　　 COOKING TIME: 10–15 minutes

nutritional information per serving	810 kcals, 30g fat, 15g sat fat, 4g total sugars, 0.3g salt

It is the pure simplicity of this delicately flavoured dish that makes it absolutely perfect.

INGREDIENTS

200 g/7 oz dried penne

1 tbsp olive oil

2 skinless, boneless chicken breasts

4 tbsp dry white wine

115 g/4 oz frozen peas

5 tbsp double cream

salt

4–5 tbsp chopped fresh parsley, to garnish

1. Bring a large saucepan of lightly salted water to the boil. Add the pasta, bring back to the boil and cook for 8–10 minutes, until tender but still firm to the bite.

2. Meanwhile, heat the oil in a frying pan, add the chicken and cook over a medium heat for about 4 minutes on each side, until cooked through and the juices run clear.

3. Pour in the wine and cook over a high heat until it has almost evaporated.

4. Drain the pasta. Add the peas, cream and pasta to the frying pan and stir well. Cover and simmer for 2 minutes. Garnish with chopped parsley and serve immediately.

1

2

4

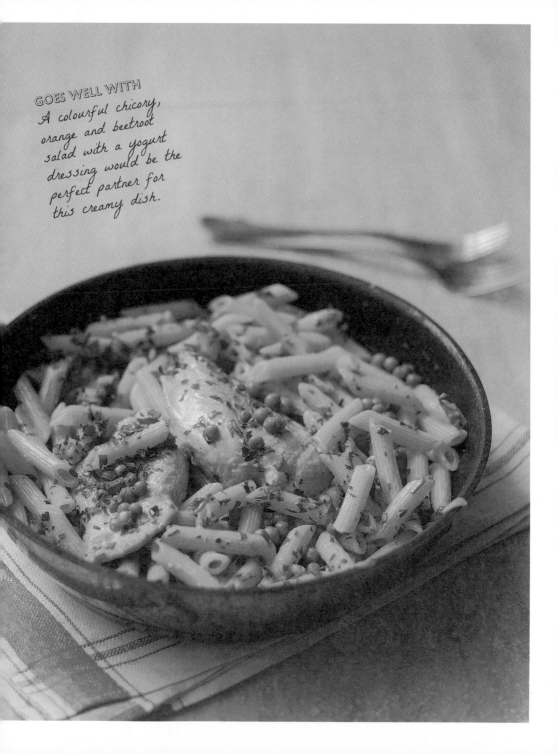

GOES WELL WITH
A colourful chicory,
orange and beetroot
salad with a yogurt
dressing would be the
perfect partner for
this creamy dish.

Tuna Pasta Bake 68

Spaghetti & Cod 70

Sicilian Swordfish Pasta 72

Linguine with Clams in Tomato Sauce 74

Tagliatelle with Smoked Salmon & Rocket 76

Penne with Squid & Tomatoes 78

Pasta Salad with Melon & Prawns 80

Salmon Lasagne Rolls 82

Spaghetti with Tuna & Parsley 84

Linguine with Prawns & Scallops 86

Spaghetti with Tuna Sauce 88

Salad Niçoise 90

Scallop Soup with Pasta 92

Mussel & Pasta Soup 94

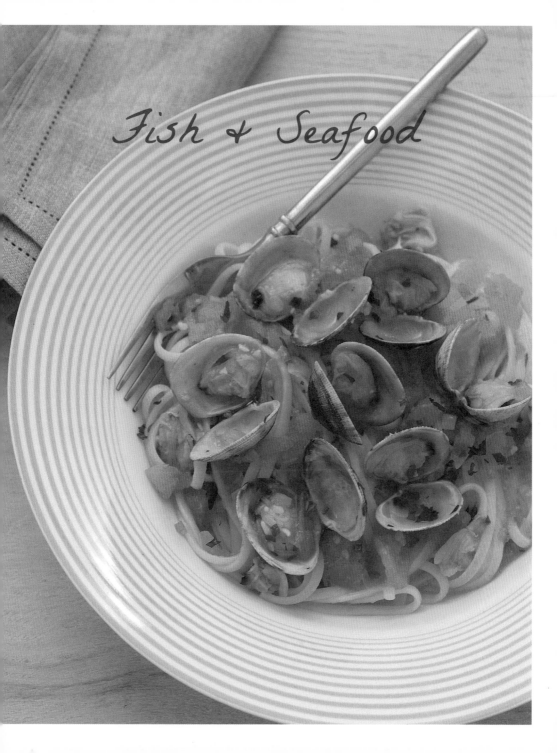

Fish & Seafood

Tuna Pasta Bake

 SERVES 4

 PREP TIME:
20 minutes

 COOKING TIME:
35 minutes

nutritional information per serving	600 kcals, 27g fat, 13g sat fat, 8g total sugars, 2.6g salt

Ever since canned condensed soups were invented in the United States in 1897, they have been used in casserole cooking. The most popular of these meals continues to be Tuna Pasta Bake.

INGREDIENTS

200 g/7 oz dried tagliatelle

25 g/1 oz butter

55 g/2 oz fresh breadcrumbs

400 ml/14 fl oz canned condensed cream of mushroom soup

125 ml/4 fl oz milk

2 celery sticks, chopped

1 red and 1 green pepper, deseeded and chopped

140 g/5 oz mature Cheddar cheese, roughly grated

2 tbsp chopped fresh parsley

200 g/7 oz canned tuna in oil, drained and flaked

salt and pepper

1. Preheat the oven to 200°C/400°F/Gas Mark 6. Bring a large pan of lightly salted water to the boil. Add the pasta and cook for 2 minutes fewer than specified on the packet instructions.

2. Meanwhile, melt the butter in a separate small saucepan over a medium heat. Stir in the breadcrumbs, then remove from the heat and reserve.

3. Drain the pasta thoroughly and reserve. Pour the soup into the pasta pan over a medium heat, then stir in the milk, celery, peppers, half the cheese and all the parsley. Add the tuna and gently stir in so that the flakes don't break up. Season to taste with salt and pepper. Heat just until small bubbles appear around the edge of the mixture – do not boil.

4. Stir the pasta into the pan and use two forks to mix all the ingredients together. Spoon the mixture into an ovenproof dish and spread out. Stir the remaining cheese into the buttered breadcrumbs, then sprinkle over the top of the pasta mixture. Bake in the preheated oven for 20–25 minutes, until golden and bubbling. Leave to stand for 5 minutes before serving.

Spaghetti & Cod

 SERVES 4

 PREP TIME:
10 minutes

 COOKING TIME:
12 minutes

nutritional information per serving	725 kcals, 39g fat, 6g sat fat, 6g total sugars, 0.3g salt

Although simplicity itself, this dish is surprisingly tasty and incredibly quick and easy to prepare and cook.

INGREDIENTS

300 g/10½ oz dried spaghetti

200 ml/7 fl oz extra virgin olive oil

1 garlic clove, peeled

450 g/1 lb cherry tomatoes, halved

pinch of crushed dried chillies (optional)

600 g/1 lb 5 oz cod fillets, skinned and cut into small chunks

salt and pepper

1. Bring a large saucepan of lightly salted water to the boil. Add the pasta, bring back to the boil and cook for 8–10 minutes, until tender but still firm to the bite. Reserve.

2. Meanwhile, put the oil into a large saucepan, add the garlic and cook over a low heat, stirring occasionally, for a few minutes until the garlic starts to brown, then remove and discard. Add the tomatoes to the pan and season with salt. Increase the heat to high and cook, tossing very occasionally, for 6–7 minutes until lightly browned and concentrated without disintegrating.

3. Add the chillies, if using, and the fish and cook, stirring gently, for 1–2 minutes. Add a ladleful of the cooking water from the pasta and taste and adjust the seasoning, if necessary. Drain the pasta, tip it into the sauce and toss together. Remove from the heat, spoon into warmed bowls and serve immediately.

SOMETHING DIFFERENT
You could substitute another firm-fleshed white fish or large peeled prawns for the cod fillet.

Sicilian Swordfish Pasta

 SERVES 4

 PREP TIME:
10 minutes

 COOKING TIME:
30 minutes

nutritional information per serving	441 kcals, 10g fat, 2g sat fat, 6.5g total sugars, 1.1g salt

Sicily is famous for its swordfish recipes, which also often include other favourite ingredients, such as capers and olives.

INGREDIENTS

1 tbsp olive oil

4 garlic cloves, peeled

1 onion, chopped

8 black olives, stoned and chopped

4 cornichons (small gherkins), chopped

2 tbsp capers in salt, rinsed and chopped

300 g/10½ oz dried spaghetti or linguine

400 g/14 oz canned chopped tomatoes

450 g/1 lb swordfish, cut into small chunks

basil leaves, to garnish

salt and pepper

1. Heat the oil in a deep frying pan and add the garlic. When the garlic begins to colour, remove and discard. Add the onion and cook over a low heat, stirring occasionally, for 8–10 minutes until light golden. Stir in the olives, cornichons and capers, season to taste with salt and pepper and cook, stirring occasionally, for 5 minutes.

2. Meanwhile, bring a large saucepan of lightly salted water to the boil. Add the pasta, bring back to the boil and cook for 8–10 minutes, until tender but still firm to the bite.

3. Add the tomatoes to the frying pan, increase the heat to medium and bring to the boil, stirring occasionally, then reduce the heat and simmer for 5 minutes. Add the swordfish chunks, cover and simmer gently for a further 5 minutes.

4. Drain the pasta and tip into a warmed serving dish. Top with the swordfish sauce and tear the basil leaves over it. Serve immediately.

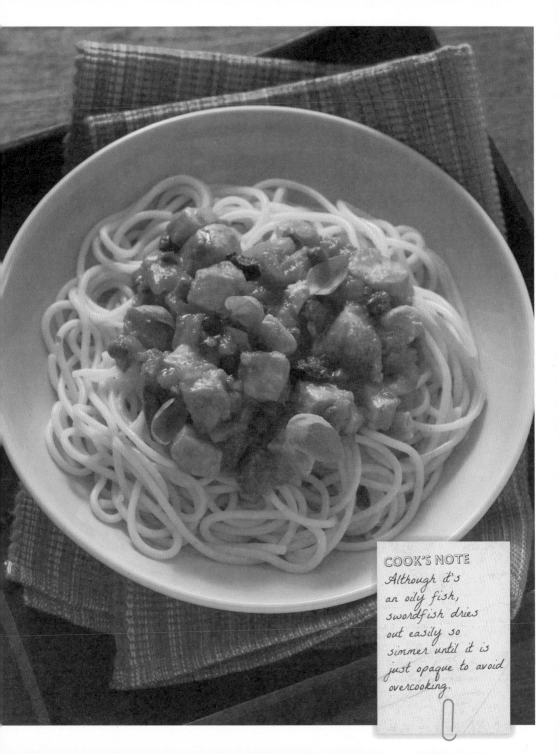

COOK'S NOTE
Although it's
an oily fish,
swordfish dries
out easily so
simmer until it is
just opaque to avoid
overcooking.

Linguine with Clams in Tomato Sauce

 SERVES 4   PREP TIME: 20 minutes   COOKING TIME: 35 minutes

nutritional information per serving	522 kcals, 11.5g fat, 2g sat fat, 9g total sugars, 0.7g salt

This Neapolitan speciality features three of the city's favourite ingredients – pasta, tomatoes and clams.

INGREDIENTS

1 kg/2 lb 4 oz live clams, scrubbed

225 ml/8 fl oz dry white wine

2 garlic cloves, roughly chopped

4 tbsp chopped fresh flat-leaf parsley

2 tbsp olive oil

1 onion, chopped

8 plum tomatoes, peeled, deseeded and chopped

1 fresh red chilli, deseeded and chopped

350 g/12 oz dried linguine

salt and pepper

1. Discard any clams with broken shells or any that refuse to close when tapped. Pour the wine into a large heavy-based saucepan and add the garlic, half the parsley and the clams. Cover and cook over a high heat, shaking the pan occasionally, for 5 minutes, or until the shells have opened. Remove the clams with a slotted spoon, reserving the cooking liquid. Discard any that remain closed and remove half of the remainder from their shells. Keep the shelled and unshelled clams in separate covered bowls. Strain the cooking liquid through a muslin-lined sieve and reserve.

2. Heat the oil in a heavy-based saucepan. Add the onion and cook over a low heat for 5 minutes, or until softened. Add the tomatoes, chilli and reserved cooking liquid and season to taste with salt and pepper. Bring to the boil, partially cover the pan and simmer for 20 minutes.

3. Meanwhile, bring a large saucepan of lightly salted water to the boil. Add the pasta, bring back to the boil and cook for 8–10 minutes, until tender but still firm to the bite. Drain and transfer to a warmed serving dish.

4. Stir the shelled clams into the tomato sauce and heat through gently for 2–3 minutes. Pour over the pasta and toss. Garnish with the clams in their shells and remaining parsley. Serve immediately.

Tagliatelle with Smoked Salmon & Rocket

 SERVES 4

 PREP TIME:
5 minutes

 COOKING TIME:
15 minutes

nutritional information
per serving | 1141 kcals, 76g fat, 44g sat fat, 5g total sugars, 2g salt

This must be one of the easiest dishes to prepare while simultaneously being one of the most delicious to eat.

INGREDIENTS

350 g/12 oz dried tagliatelle
2 tbsp olive oil
1 garlic clove, finely chopped
115 g/4 oz smoked salmon,
cut into thin strips
55 g/2 oz rocket
salt and pepper

1. Bring a large saucepan of lightly salted water to the boil. Add the pasta, bring back to the boil and cook for 8–10 minutes, until tender but still firm to the bite.

2. Just before the end of the cooking time, heat the olive oil in a heavy-based frying pan. Add the garlic and cook over a low heat, stirring constantly, for 1 minute. Do not allow the garlic to brown or it will taste bitter.

3. Add the salmon and rocket. Season to taste with pepper and cook, stirring constantly, for 1 minute. Remove the frying pan from the heat.

4. Drain the pasta and transfer to a warmed serving dish. Add the smoked salmon and rocket mixture, toss lightly and serve immediately.

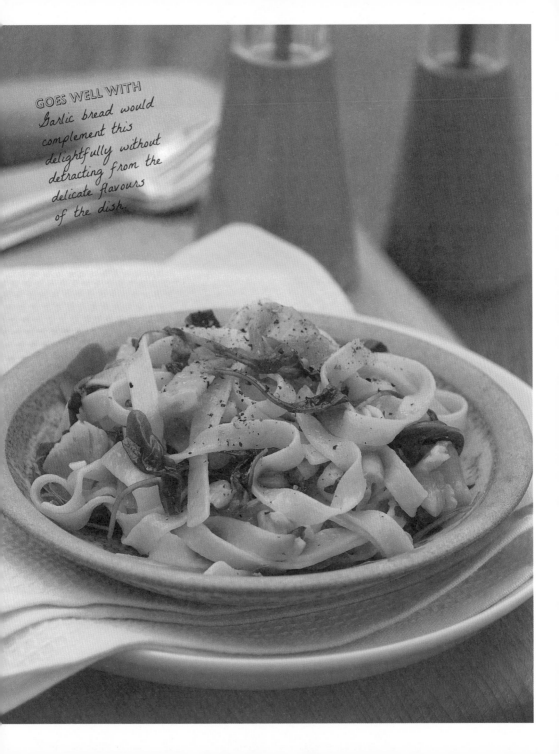

GOES WELL WITH
Garlic bread would
complement this
delightfully without
detracting from the
delicate flavours
of the dish.

Penne with Squid & Tomatoes

 SERVES 4   PREP TIME: 15 minutes   COOKING TIME: 25–30 minutes

nutritional information per serving	493 kcals, 19g fat, 3g sat fat, 8g total sugars, 0.6g salt

The availability of prepared squid makes this richly flavoured southern Italian dish quick and trouble-free.

INGREDIENTS

225 g/8 oz dried penne

350 g/12 oz prepared squid

6 tbsp olive oil

2 onions, sliced

225 ml/8 fl oz fish or chicken stock

150 ml/5 fl oz full-bodied red wine

400 g/14 oz canned chopped tomatoes

2 tbsp tomato purée

1 tbsp chopped fresh marjoram

1 bay leaf

salt and pepper

2 tbsp chopped fresh parsley, to garnish

1. Bring a large saucepan of lightly salted water to the boil. Add the pasta, bring back to the boil and cook for 3 minutes, then drain and reserve until required. With a sharp knife, cut the squid into strips.

2. Heat the oil in a large saucepan. Add the onions and cook over a low heat, stirring occasionally, for 5 minutes, or until softened. Add the squid and stock, bring to the boil and simmer for 3 minutes. Stir in the wine, tomatoes and their can juices, tomato purée, marjoram and bay leaf. Season to taste with salt and pepper. Bring to the boil and cook for 5 minutes, or until slightly reduced.

3. Add the pasta, return to the boil and simmer for 5–7 minutes, or until the pasta is tender but still firm to the bite. Remove and discard the bay leaf. Transfer to a warmed serving dish, garnish with the parsley and serve immediately.

Pasta Salad with Melon & Prawns

 SERVES 6

 PREP TIME: 25 minutes plus chilling

 COOKING TIME: 10 minutes

nutritional information per serving	334 kcals, 11g fat, 1.5g sat fat, 15g total sugars, 1.2g salt

This lovely salad looks really spectacular and tastes fabulous so would be a great choice for a special occasion.

INGREDIENTS

225 g/8 oz dried green fusilli
5 tbsp extra virgin olive oil
450 g/1 lb cooked prawns
1 Charentais melon
1 Galia melon
1 tbsp red wine vinegar
1 tsp Dijon mustard
pinch of caster sugar
1 tbsp chopped fresh flat-leaf parsley
1 tbsp chopped fresh basil, plus extra sprigs to garnish
1 oakleaf or quattro stagioni lettuce, shredded
salt and pepper

1. Bring a large saucepan of lightly salted water to the boil. Add the pasta, bring back to the boil and cook for 8–10 minutes, until tender but still firm to the bite. Drain, toss with 1 tablespoon of the oil and leave to cool.

2. Meanwhile, peel and devein the prawns, then place them in a large bowl. Halve both the melons and scoop out the seeds with a spoon. Using a melon baller or teaspoon, scoop out balls of the flesh and add them to the prawns.

3. Whisk together the remaining oil, the vinegar, mustard, sugar, parsley and basil in a small bowl. Season to taste with salt and pepper. Add the cooled pasta to the prawn and melon mixture and toss lightly to mix, then pour in the dressing and toss again. Cover with clingfilm and chill in the refrigerator for 30 minutes.

4. Make a bed of shredded lettuce on a serving plate. Spoon the pasta salad on top, garnish with basil sprigs and serve immediately.

2

2

3

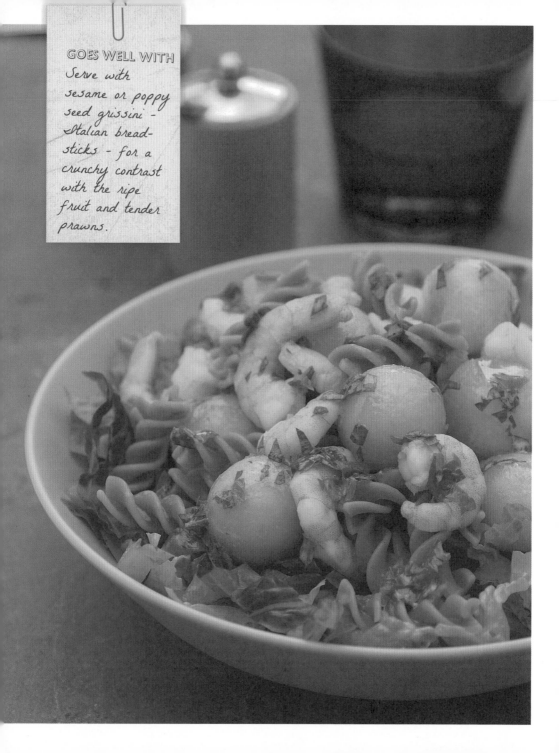

GOES WELL WITH
Serve with sesame or poppy seed grissini - Italian breadsticks - for a crunchy contrast with the ripe fruit and tender prawns.

Salmon Lasagne Rolls

 SERVES 4

 PREP TIME
15 minutes

 COOKING TIME
1 hour

nutritional information per serving	487 kcals, 22g fat, 9g sat fat, 9g total sugars, 0.6g salt

This attractive and colourful dish is much easier to make than you might think and is well worth a little extra time.

INGREDIENTS

8 sheets dried lasagne verde

25 g/1 oz butter

1 onion, sliced

½ red pepper, deseeded and chopped

1 courgette, diced

1 tsp chopped fresh ginger

125 g/4½ oz oyster mushrooms, torn into pieces

225 g/8 oz salmon fillet, skinned and cut into chunks

3 tbsp dry sherry

2 tsp cornflour

vegetable oil, for brushing

3 tbsp plain flour

425 ml/15 fl oz milk

25 g/1 oz finely grated Cheddar cheese

1 tbsp fresh white breadcrumbs

salt and pepper

1. Bring a large saucepan of lightly salted water to the boil. Add the pasta, bring back to the boil and cook for 8–10 minutes, until tender but still firm to the bite. Remove with tongs and drain on a clean tea towel.

2. Melt half the butter in a saucepan. Add the onion and cook over a low heat, stirring occasionally, for 5 minutes, until softened. Add the red pepper, courgette and ginger and cook, stirring occasionally, for 10 minutes. Add the mushrooms and salmon and cook for 2 minutes, then mix together the sherry and cornflour and stir into the pan. Cook for a further 4 minutes, until the fish is opaque and flakes easily. Season to taste with salt and pepper and remove the pan from the heat.

3. Preheat the oven to 200°C/400°F/Gas Mark 6. Brush an ovenproof dish with oil.

4. Melt the remaining butter in another pan. Stir in the flour and cook, stirring constantly, for 2 minutes. Gradually stir in the milk, then cook, stirring constantly, for 10 minutes. Remove the pan from the heat, stir in half the Cheddar cheese and season to taste with salt and pepper.

5. Spoon the salmon filling along one of the shorter sides of each sheet of lasagne. Roll up and place in the prepared dish. Pour the sauce over the rolls and sprinkle with the breadcrumbs and remaining cheese. Bake in the preheated oven for 15–20 minutes, until golden and bubbling. Serve immediately.

Spaghetti with Tuna & Parsley

 SERVES 4   PREP TIME: 10 minutes   COOKING TIME: 15 minutes

nutritional information per serving	1109 kcals, 70g fat, 21g sat fat, 5g total sugars, 1.6g salt

This tasty dish is a great storecupboard stand-by that can be rustled up in no time at all.

INGREDIENTS

500 g/1 lb 2 oz dried spaghetti

25 g/1 oz butter

200 g/7 oz canned tuna in spring water, drained

55 g/2 oz canned anchovies, drained

250 ml/9 fl oz olive oil

1 large bunch of fresh flat-leaf parsley, roughly chopped

150 ml/5 fl oz crème fraîche

salt and pepper

1. Bring a large saucepan of lightly salted water to the boil. Add the pasta, bring back to the boil and cook for 8–10 minutes, until tender but still firm to the bite. Drain the spaghetti in a colander and return to the pan. Add the butter, toss thoroughly to coat and keep warm until required.

2. Flake the tuna into smaller pieces using two forks. Place the tuna in a food processor or blender with the anchovies, oil and parsley and process until the sauce is smooth. Pour in the crème fraîche and process for a few seconds to blend. Taste the sauce and season to taste with salt and pepper, if necessary.

3. Shake the pan of spaghetti over a medium heat for a few minutes, or until it is thoroughly warmed.

4. Pour the sauce over the spaghetti and toss. Serve immediately.

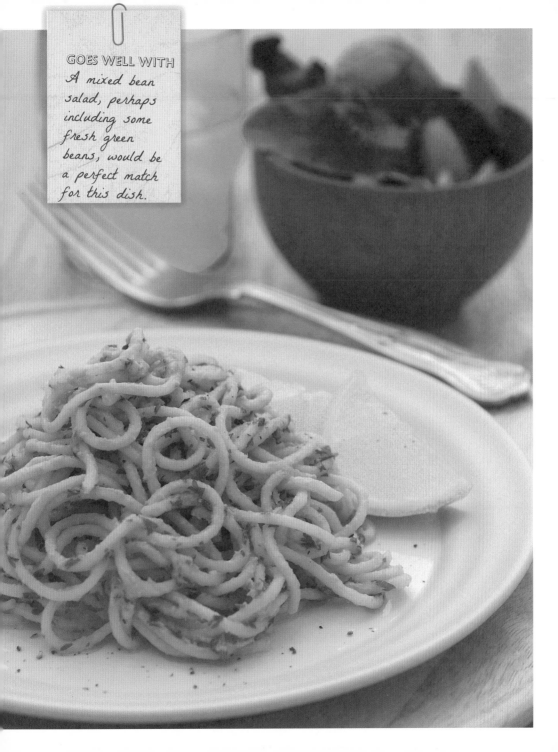

GOES WELL WITH
A mixed bean salad, perhaps including some fresh green beans, would be a perfect match for this dish.

Linguine with Prawns & Scallops

 SERVES 6

 PREP TIME:
15 minutes

 COOKING TIME:
25–30 minutes

nutritional information per serving	514 kcals, 10g fat, 3g sat fat, 3g total sugars, 0.8g salt

This impressive dish from the coastal regions of northern Italy is a real treat for lovers of seafood.

INGREDIENTS

450 g/1 lb raw prawns

25 g/1 oz butter

2 shallots, finely chopped

225 ml/8 fl oz dry white vermouth

350 ml/12 fl oz water

450 g/1 lb dried linguine

2 tbsp olive oil

450 g/1 lb prepared scallops, thawed if frozen

2 tbsp snipped fresh chives

salt and pepper

1. Peel and devein the prawns, reserving the shells. Melt the butter in a heavy-based frying pan. Add the shallots and cook over a low heat, stirring occasionally, for 5 minutes, or until softened. Add the prawn shells and cook, stirring constantly, for 1 minute. Pour in the vermouth and cook, stirring, for 1 minute. Add the water, bring to the boil, then reduce the heat and simmer for 10 minutes, or until the liquid has reduced by half. Remove the pan from the heat.

2. Bring a large saucepan of lightly salted water to the boil. Add the pasta, bring back to the boil and cook for 8–10 minutes, until tender but still firm to the bite.

3. Meanwhile, heat the oil in a separate heavy-based frying pan. Add the scallops and prawns and cook, stirring frequently, for 2 minutes, or until the scallops are opaque and the prawns have changed colour. Strain the prawn-shell stock into the frying pan. Drain the pasta and add to the frying pan with the chives. Season to taste with salt and pepper. Toss well over a low heat for 1 minute, then serve.

1

1

3

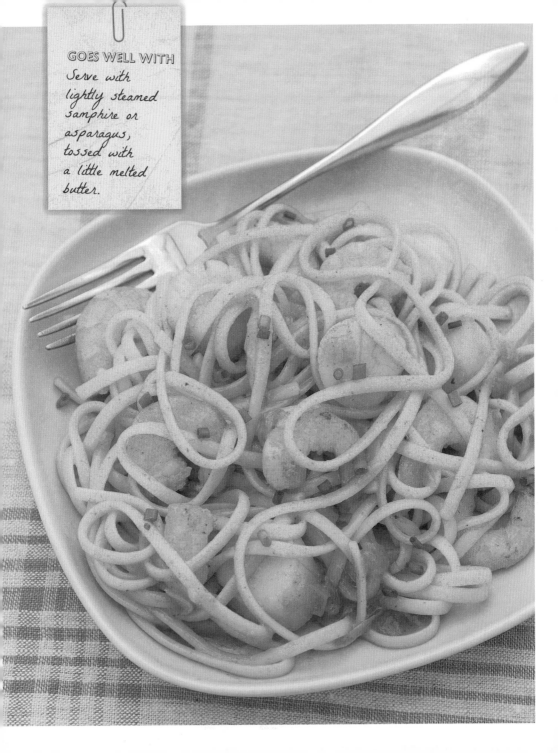

GOES WELL WITH
Serve with
lightly steamed
samphire or
asparagus,
tossed with
a little melted
butter.

Spaghetti with Tuna Sauce

 SERVES 4

 PREP TIME: 10 minutes

 COOKING TIME: 15 minutes

nutritional information per serving	493 kcals, 8g fat, 1g sat fat, 8g total sugars, 0.8g salt

This is a terrific stand-by dish for those times when you have run out of ideas or are simply feeling tired.

INGREDIENTS

350 g/12 oz dried spaghetti

2 tbsp olive oil

1 garlic clove, peeled

1 onion, chopped

500 g/1 lb 2 oz tomatoes, chopped

400 g/14 oz canned tuna in spring water, drained and flaked

2 tbsp capers, rinsed (optional)

2 tbsp chopped fresh parsley, or 1 tbsp chopped fresh basil or pinch of dried oregano

salt and pepper

1. Bring a large saucepan of lightly salted water to the boil. Add the pasta, bring back to the boil and cook for 8–10 minutes, until tender but still firm to the bite.

2. Meanwhile, heat the oil in a separate saucepan and add the garlic. When it has begun to colour, remove and discard it. Add the onion and tomatoes to the pan and cook over a low heat, stirring occasionally, for 5 minutes.

3. Drain the pasta and tip it into the pan with the tomato mixture. Add the tuna and capers, if using, and toss over the heat for a few minutes until heated through. Remove from the heat, season to taste with salt and pepper, stir in the herbs and serve immediately.

1

2

3

SOMETHING DIFFERENT

You can add extra ingredients, such as a few chopped canned anchovies or sliced stoned olives, depending on what you have to hand.

Salad Niçoise

 SERVES 6   PREP TIME: 10 minutes   COOKING TIME: 10–15 minutes

nutritional information per serving	405 kcals, 14g fat, 3g sat fat, 4g total sugars, 1.2g salt

It is a matter of debate in culinary circles whether this Mediterranean salad should contain tomatoes, green beans, or hard-boiled eggs, but most contain all these ingredients.

INGREDIENTS

350 g/12 oz dried conchiglie

2 tuna steaks, about 2 cm/¾ inch thick

olive oil, for brushing

250 g/9 oz French beans, topped and tailed

shop-bought garlic vinaigrette, to taste

2 hearts of lettuce, leaves separated

3 large hard-boiled eggs, halved

2 juicy tomatoes, cut into wedges

50 g/1¾ oz anchovy fillets in oil, drained

55 g/2 oz pitted black or Niçoise olives

salt and pepper

1. Bring a large saucepan of lightly salted water to the boil. Add the pasta, bring back to the boil and cook for 8–10 minutes, until tender but still firm to the bite. Drain and refresh in cold water.

2. Heat a ridged cast-iron griddle pan over a high heat. Brush the tuna steaks with oil on one side, place oiled-side down on the hot pan and chargrill for 2 minutes.

3. Lightly brush the top side of the tuna steaks with a little more oil. Turn the tuna steaks over, then season to taste with salt and pepper. Continue chargrilling for a further 2 minutes for rare or up to 4 minutes for well done. Leave to cool.

4. Meanwhile, bring a large saucepan of lightly salted water to the boil. Add the beans and return to the boil, then boil for 3 minutes. Drain and immediately transfer to a large bowl. Pour over the garlic vinaigrette and stir together.

5. To serve, line a serving dish with lettuce leaves. Lift the beans out of the bowl, leaving the excess dressing behind, and pile them in the centre of the platter. Break the tuna into large flakes and arrange it over the beans.

6. Arrange the hard-boiled eggs, tomatoes, anchovy fillets and olives on the platter. Drizzle over more vinaigrette, if required, and serve immediately.

Scallop Soup with Pasta

 SERVES 6

 PREP TIME:
15 minutes

 COOKING TIME:
10–15 minutes

nutritional information per serving	444 kcals, 15g fat, 8g sat fat, 5g total sugars, 1.6g salt

If you're planning a formal dinner party, this elegant soup would be an ideal first course.

INGREDIENTS

500 g/1 lb 2 oz shelled scallops

350 ml/12 fl oz milk

1.5 litres/2¾ pints vegetable stock

250 g/9 oz frozen petits pois

175 g/6 oz dried taglialini

70 g/2½ oz butter

2 spring onions, finely chopped

175 ml/6 fl oz dry white wine

3 slices of prosciutto, cut into thin strips

salt and pepper

chopped fresh flat-leaf parsley, to garnish

crusty baguette, to serve

1. Slice the scallops in half horizontally and season to taste with salt and pepper.

2. Pour the milk and stock into a saucepan, add a pinch of salt and bring to the boil. Add the petits pois and pasta, bring back to the boil and cook for 8–10 minutes, until the pasta is tender but still firm to the bite.

3. Meanwhile, melt the butter in a frying pan. Add the spring onions and cook over a low heat, stirring occasionally, for 3 minutes. Add the scallops and cook for 45 seconds on each side. Pour in the wine, add the prosciutto and cook for 2–3 minutes.

4. Stir the scallop mixture into the soup, taste and adjust the seasoning, if necessary, and garnish with the parsley. Serve immediately with the baguette.

1

2

3

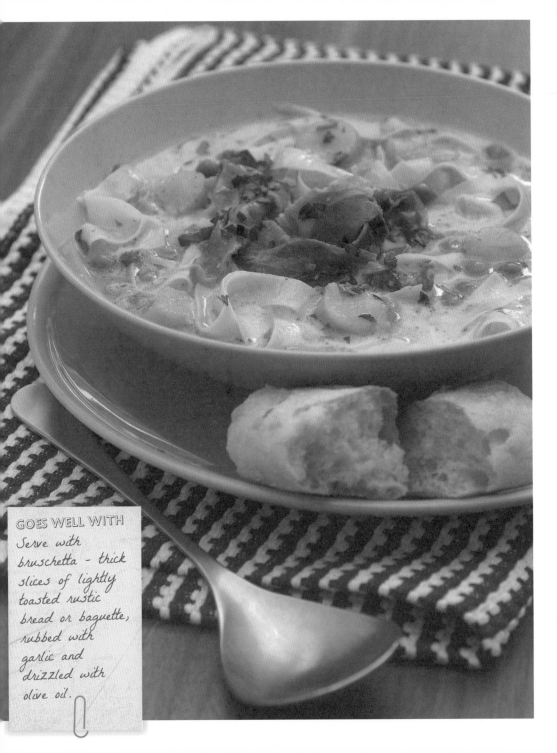

GOES WELL WITH
Serve with
bruschetta - thick
slices of lightly
toasted rustic
bread or baguette,
rubbed with
garlic and
drizzled with
olive oil.

Mussel & Pasta Soup

 SERVES 4

 PREP TIME:
15 minutes

 COOKING TIME:
35 minutes

nutritional information per serving	996 kcals, 75g fat, 41g sat fat, 4g total sugars, 1.3g salt

This rich and filling soup is full of flavour and would make a great weekend lunch with some crusty bread.

INGREDIENTS

750 g/1 lb 10 oz mussels, scrubbed and debearded

2 tbsp olive oil

100 g/3½ oz butter

55 g/2 oz rindless streaky bacon, chopped

1 onion, chopped

2 garlic cloves, finely chopped

55 g/2 oz plain flour

3 potatoes, thinly sliced

115 g/4 oz dried farfalle

300 ml/10 fl oz double cream

1 tbsp lemon juice

2 egg yolks

salt and pepper

2 tbsp finely chopped fresh parsley, to garnish

1. Discard any mussels with broken shells or any that refuse to close when tapped. Bring a large heavy-based saucepan of water to the boil. Add the mussels and oil and season to taste with pepper. Cover tightly and cook over a high heat for 5 minutes, or until the mussels have opened. Remove the mussels with a slotted spoon, discarding any that remain closed. Strain the cooking liquid through a muslin-lined sieve and reserve 1.2 litres/2 pints.

2. Melt the butter in a saucepan. Add the bacon, onion and garlic and cook over a low heat, stirring occasionally, for 5 minutes. Stir in the flour and cook, stirring, for 1 minute. Gradually stir in all but 2 tablespoons of the reserved cooking liquid and bring to the boil, stirring constantly. Add the potato slices and simmer for 5 minutes. Add the pasta and simmer for a further 10 minutes.

3. Stir in the cream and lemon juice and season to taste with salt and pepper. Add the mussels. Mix the egg yolks and the remaining mussel cooking liquid together, then stir the mixture into the soup and cook for 4 minutes, until thickened.

4. Ladle the soup into warmed bowls, garnish with chopped parsley and serve immediately.

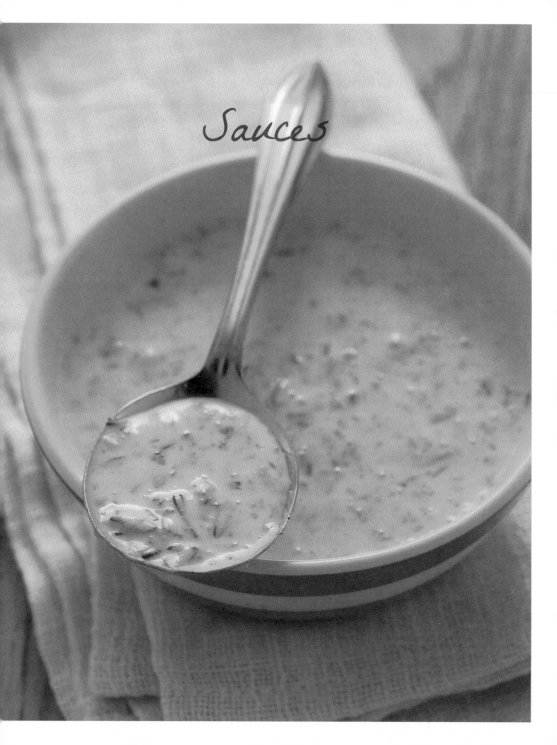

Sauces

Basic Tomato Sauce

 SERVES 4

 PREP TIME:
10 minutes

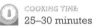 COOKING TIME:
25–30 minutes

nutritional information per serving	124 kcals, 11g fat, 4g sat fat, 5g total sugars, 0.2g salt

There is no question that this is Italy's absolute favourite sauce for serving with pasta as well as other ingredients.

INGREDIENTS

25 g/1 oz butter

2 tbsp olive oil

1 onion, finely chopped

1 garlic clove, finely chopped

1 celery stick, finely chopped

400 g/14 oz canned chopped tomatoes or 500 g/1 lb 2 oz plum tomatoes, peeled, cored and chopped

2 tbsp tomato purée

brown sugar, to taste

1 tbsp chopped fresh herbs and/ or 1–2 tsp dried herbs and/ or 1–2 bay leaves

100 ml/3½ fl oz water

salt and pepper

1. Melt the butter with the oil in a saucepan. Add the onion, garlic and celery and cook over a low heat, stirring occasionally, for 5 minutes, until softened.

2. Stir in the tomatoes, tomato purée, sugar to taste, the herbs and water and season to taste with salt and pepper.

3. Increase the heat to medium and bring to the boil, then reduce the heat and simmer, stirring occasionally, for 15–20 minutes, until thickened. Remove the bay leaves, if using. Use as required.

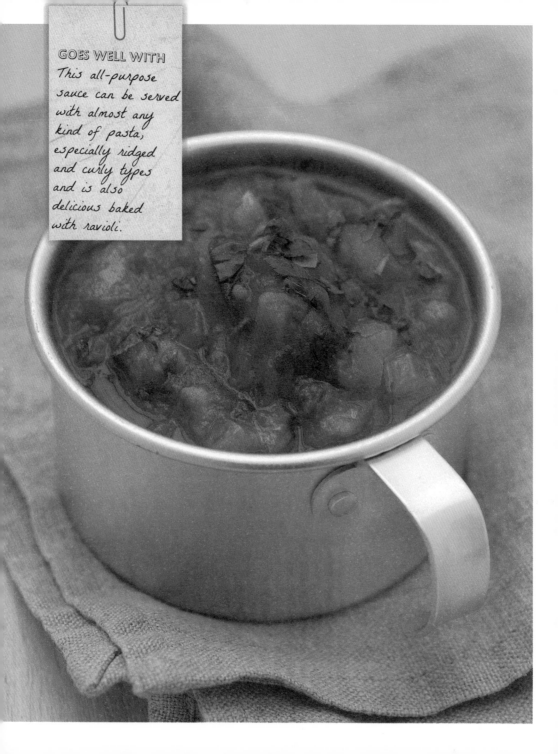

GOES WELL WITH
This all-purpose sauce can be served with almost any kind of pasta, especially ridged and curly types and is also delicious baked with ravioli.

Classic Pesto

 SERVES 4

 PREP TIME:
10 minutes

 COOKING TIME:
No cooking

nutritional information per serving	144 kcals, 13.5g fat, 3.5g sat fat, 0.3g total sugars, 0.2g salt

Pesto is delicious stirred into pasta, soups and salad dressings. It is available in most supermarkets, but making your own gives a concentrated flavour.

INGREDIENTS

40 fresh basil leaves

3 garlic cloves, crushed

25 g/1 oz pine nuts

50 g/1¾ oz Parmesan cheese, finely grated

2–3 tbsp extra virgin olive oil

salt and pepper

1. Rinse the basil leaves and pat them dry with kitchen paper. Put the basil leaves, garlic, pine nuts and cheese into a food processor or blender and blend for 30 seconds or until smooth. Alternatively, pound all of the ingredients in a mortar with a pestle.

2. If you are using a food processor, keep the motor running and slowly add the olive oil. Alternatively, add the oil drop by drop while stirring briskly. Season with salt and pepper to taste. Use as required.

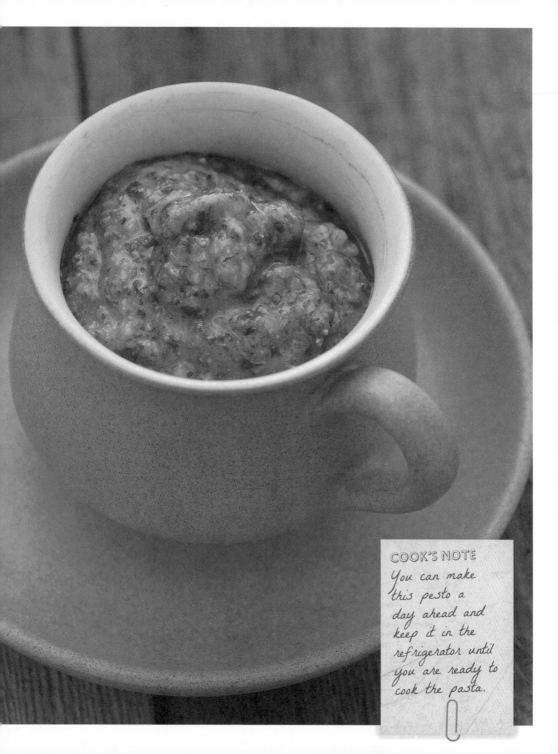

Roasted Garlic & Herb Sauce

 SERVES 4   PREP TIME: 10 minutes   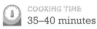 COOKING TIME: 35–40 minutes

nutritional information per serving	72 kcals, 5g fat, 2g sat fat, 1g total sugars, trace salt

Roasting garlic gives it a wonderfully mild flavour and a deliciously creamy texture.

INGREDIENTS

1 garlic bulb

1 tbsp olive oil

2 handfuls of mixed herbs, such as flat-leaf parsley, basil, thyme and sage, coarse stalks removed

3–4 tbsp soured cream

salt and pepper

1. Preheat the oven to 200°C/400°F/Gas Mark 6. Peel the outer papery layers from the garlic bulb but leave the individual cloves intact. Using a sharp knife, cut a 5–10-mm/¼–½-inch slice off the top of the garlic to expose the cloves.

2. Put the bulb into a small ovenproof dish, such as a ramekin, and drizzle with the oil. Cover with foil and roast in the preheated oven for 35–40 minutes until the cloves feel soft.

3. Remove from the oven and leave until cool enough to handle, then squeeze out the pulp from each clove into a food processor or blender. Add the herbs and soured cream and process until combined and reheat the sauce gently over a low heat without boiling, if required. Season to taste with salt and pepper and use as required.

2

2

3

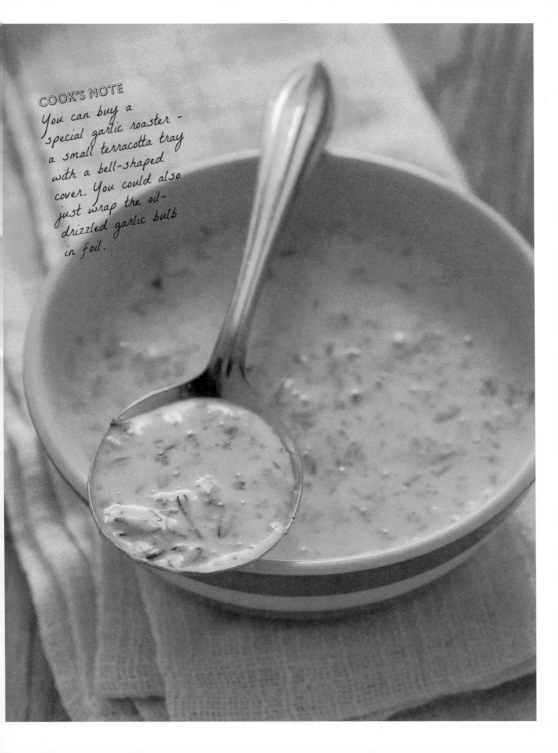

COOK'S NOTE
You can buy a special garlic roaster - a small terracotta tray with a bell-shaped cover. You could also just wrap the oil-drizzled garlic bulb in foil.

Simple Butter Sauce

 SERVES 4   PREP TIME: 10 minutes   COOKING TIME: 15 minutes

nutritional information per serving	562 kcals, 26g fat, 15g sat fat, 2g total sugars, 0.5g salt

Fresh-tasting and made in minutes, this is a great way to serve any long pasta, such as linguine, for a midweek family meal.

INGREDIENTS

400 g/14 oz dried long pasta
115 g/4 oz butter
8 sage leaves, finely chopped
8 basil leaves, finely chopped
½ bunch fresh flat-leaf parsley, finely chopped
6 fresh thyme sprigs, finely chopped
1 small bunch of chives, snipped
salt and pepper
freshly grated Parmesan cheese, to serve

1. Bring a large saucepan of lightly salted water to the boil. Add the pasta, bring back to the boil and cook for 8–10 minutes, until tender but still firm to the bite.

2. Just before the pasta is ready, melt the butter in a frying pan over a low heat. Drain the pasta and pour the melted butter into the pan with the pasta. Add all the herbs, season to taste with salt and pepper and toss until the pasta strands are coated and glistening.

3. Divide between warmed plates and serve immediately, with the Parmesan cheese handed separately.

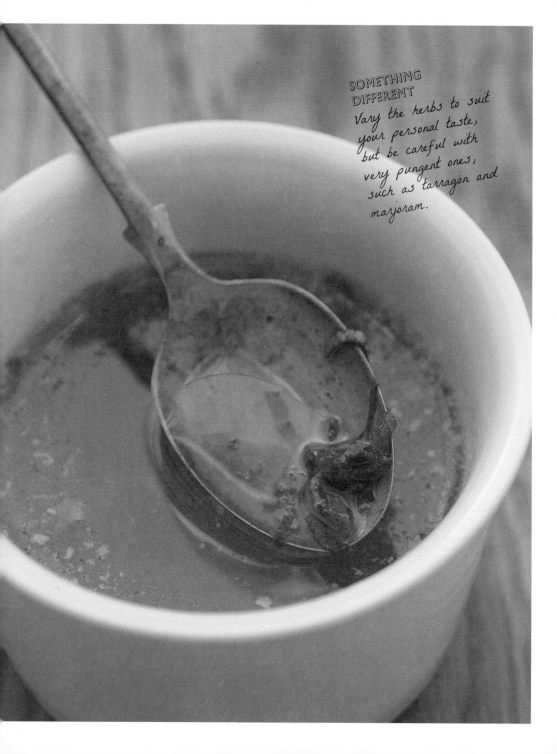

SOMETHING
DIFFERENT
Vary the herbs to suit
your personal taste,
but be careful with
very pungent ones,
such as tarragon and
marjoram.

Lemon & Tarragon Sauce

 SERVES 4

 PREP TIME:
10 minutes

 COOKING TIME:
No cooking

nutritional information per serving	200 kcals, 12g fat, 2g sat fat, 0.5g total sugars, trace salt

The sharpness of lemon and the hint of aniseed in tarragon make this a really refreshing combination.

INGREDIENTS

1 small bunch of tarragon
juice of ½ lemon
grated rind of 1 lemon
4 tbsp olive oil
2 garlic cloves, coarsely chopped
4 fresh parsley sprigs
1 bunch of chives
salt

1. Pick off the leaves from the tarragon and put them into a food processor or blender with the lemon juice, lemon rind, oil, garlic, parsley, chives and a generous pinch of salt and process until thoroughly combined. Use as required.

SOMETHING
DIFFERENT
For a sweeter flavour,
substitute 2 tablespoons
of orange juice and the
grated rind of ½ an
orange for the lemon
juice and rind.

Creole Sauce

 SERVES 4   PREP TIME 15 minutes   COOKING TIME 35–40 minutes

nutritional information per serving	127 kcals, 6.5g fat, 1g sat fat, 10g total sugars, 0.2g salt

Enjoy a taste of the Deep South with this vibrant, spicy sauce, the chopped okra lending it both characteristic flavour and thickness.

INGREDIENTS

2 tbsp sunflower oil

1 red pepper, deseeded and thinly sliced

1 green pepper, deseeded and thinly sliced

1 onion, thinly sliced

2–3 garlic cloves, crushed

1 fresh red chilli, deseeded and chopped

1 tsp ground coriander

1 tsp ground cumin

450 g/1 lb ripe tomatoes, peeled and chopped

300 ml/10 fl oz vegetable stock

115 g/4 oz okra, trimmed and chopped

1 tbsp chopped fresh coriander

salt and pepper

1. Heat the oil in a heavy-based saucepan, add the red pepper, green pepper, onion, garlic and chilli and sauté, stirring frequently, for 3 minutes. Add the ground coriander and cumin and sauté, stirring frequently, for a further 3 minutes.

2. Stir in the tomatoes and stock and bring to the boil. Reduce the heat and simmer, stirring occasionally, for 15 minutes, or until the sauce has reduced slightly.

3. Add the okra to the pan with salt and pepper to taste and simmer for a further 10–15 minutes, or until the sauce has thickened. Stir in the fresh coriander and use as required.

Four Cheese Sauce

 SERVES 4   PREP TIME 10 minutes   COOKING TIME 8–10 minutes

nutritional information per serving	879 kcals, 44g fat, 27g sat fat, 2.5g total sugars, 2.5g salt

Unusually, this sauce is actually made in the serving dish containing the drained pasta and must be one of the quickest ever!

INGREDIENTS

450 g/1 lb dried tagliatelle

55 g/2 oz butter

100 g/3½ oz Gorgonzola, crumbled

100 g/3½ oz fontina cheese, cut into narrow julienne strips

100 g/3½ oz Gruyère cheese, cut into julienne strips

100 g/3½ oz Parmesan cheese, cut into julienne strips

salt

1. Bring a large saucepan of lightly salted water to the boil. Add the pasta, bring back to the boil and cook for 8–10 minutes, until tender but still firm to the bite.

2. Meanwhile, put the butter in a heatproof bowl set over a saucepan of barely simmering water. When it has melted, continue to heat it until very hot, but not boiling.

3. Drain the pasta and tip into a warmed serving bowl. Sprinkle with the four cheeses and pour the hot butter over. Toss lightly and serve immediately.

1

2

3

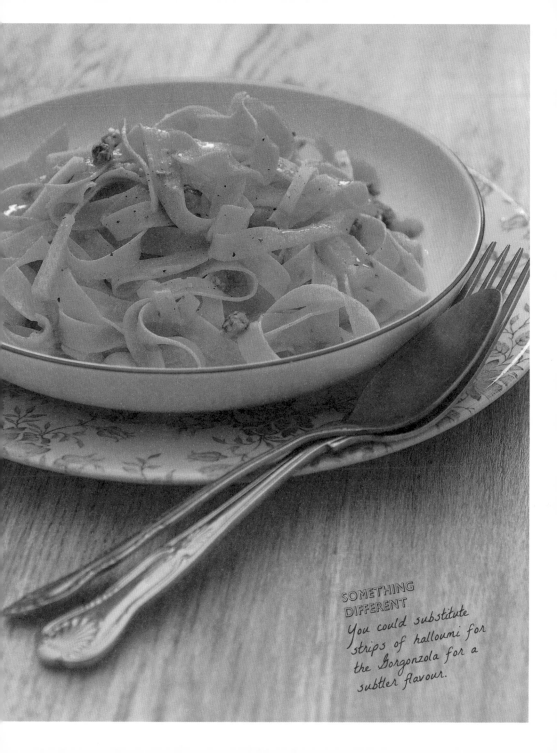

SOMETHING
DIFFERENT
You could substitute
strips of halloumi for
the Gorgonzola for a
subtler flavour.

Red Wine Sauce

 SERVES 4

 PREP TIME: 10 minutes

 COOKING TIME: 20 minutes

nutritional information per serving	240 kcals, 20g fat, 10g sat fat, 2.5g total sugars, 0.6g salt

Mushrooms are more usually cooked with white wine, but the robust earthy flavour of wild mushrooms is perfectly complemented by red wine in this sauce.

INGREDIENTS

70–100 g/2½–3½ oz butter

350 g/12 oz mixed wild mushrooms, halved or quartered if large

2 garlic cloves, finely chopped

1 tbsp olive oil

4 tbsp tomato purée

250 ml/9 fl oz full-bodied red wine

50 g/1¾ oz black olives, stoned and halved

1 tbsp chopped fresh parsley

salt and pepper

1. Melt 25 g/1 oz of the butter in a large frying pan, add the mushrooms, sprinkle with a little salt and cook over a high heat, stirring occasionally, for 5 minutes.

2. Reduce the heat under the frying pan to low, stir in the garlic and oil and cook for 2 minutes, then stir in the tomato purée and cook for a further 2 minutes.

3. Pour in the wine and cook for about 5 minutes until the alcohol has evaporated. Meanwhile, dice the remaining butter. Add the butter to the pan, 1 piece at a time, gently swirling the pan until the butter has melted. Stir in the olives, season to taste with salt and pepper and remove the pan from the heat. Sprinkle with parsley and use as required.

Sun-dried Tomato Sauce

 SERVES 4   PREP TIME: 10 minutes   COOKING TIME: 15–20 minutes

nutritional information per serving	600 kcals, 18g fat, 1.5g sat fat, 13g total sugars, 0.2g salt

Sun-dried tomatoes give this almost instant sauce intense depth and sweetness.

INGREDIENTS

3 tbsp olive oil

2 large onions, sliced

2 celery sticks, thinly sliced

2 garlic cloves, chopped

400 g/14 oz canned chopped tomatoes

125 g/4½ oz sun-dried tomatoes in oil, drained and chopped

2 tbsp tomato purée

1 tbsp dark muscovado sugar

about 150 ml/5 fl oz white wine or water

salt and pepper

1. Heat the oil in a frying pan. Add the onions and celery and cook until translucent. Add the garlic and cook for 1 minute. Stir in all the tomatoes, tomato purée, sugar and wine and season to taste with salt and pepper. Bring to the boil and simmer for 10 minutes. Use as required.

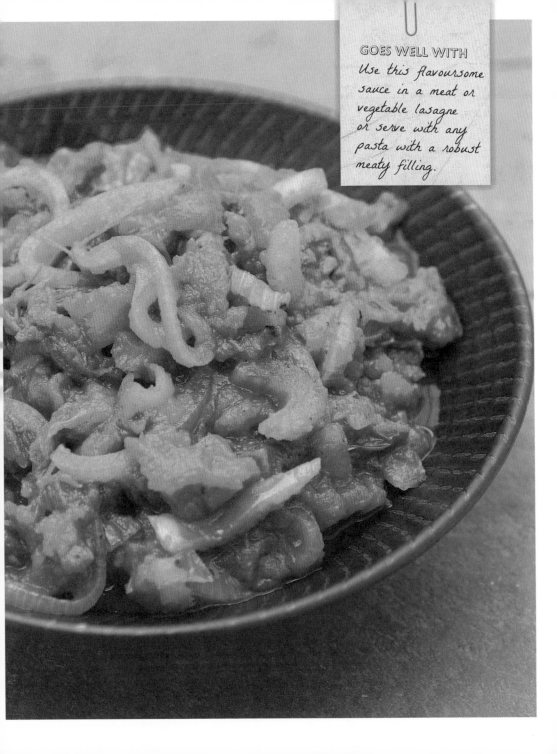

GOES WELL WITH
Use this flavoursome
sauce in a meat or
vegetable lasagne
or serve with any
pasta with a robust
meaty filling.

Mushroom Sauce

SERVES 4

PREP TIME:
10 minutes

COOKING TIME:
20 minutes

nutritional information per serving	746 kcals, 43g fat, 20g sat fat, 5g total sugars, 0.3g salt

This is a delicious sauce which uses shallots, chestnut mushrooms, double cream and port for a truly luxurious touch.

INGREDIENTS

55 g/2 oz butter
1 tbsp olive oil
6 shallots, sliced
450 g/1 lb chestnut mushrooms, sliced
1 tsp plain flour
150 ml/5 fl oz double cream
2 tbsp port
115 g/4 oz sun-dried tomatoes in oil, drained and chopped
pinch of freshly grated nutmeg
salt and pepper

1. Melt the butter with the oil in a large heavy-based frying pan. Add the shallots and cook over a low heat, stirring occasionally, for 4–5 minutes, or until softened. Add the mushrooms and cook over a low heat for a further 2 minutes. Season to taste with salt and pepper, sprinkle in the flour and cook, stirring, for 1 minute.

2. Remove the frying pan from the heat and gradually stir in the cream and port. Return to the heat, add the sun-dried tomatoes and grated nutmeg and cook over a low heat, stirring occasionally, for 8 minutes. Use as required.

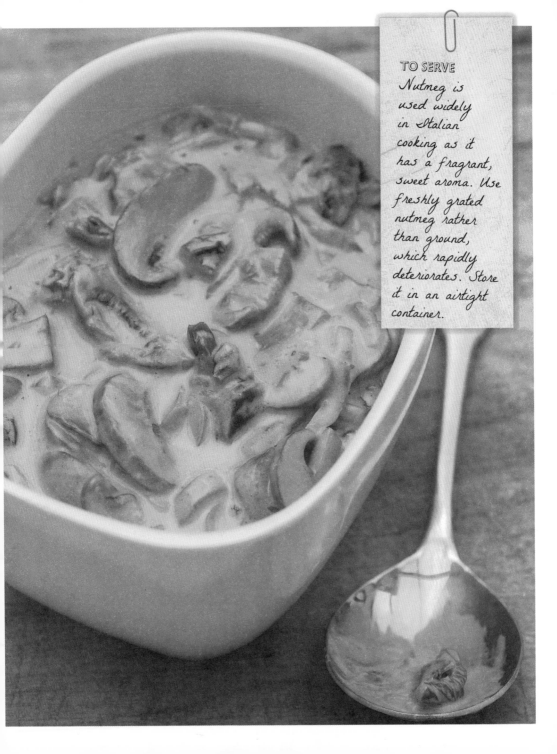

TO SERVE
Nutmeg is used widely in Italian cooking as it has a fragrant, sweet aroma. Use freshly grated nutmeg rather than ground, which rapidly deteriorates. Store it in an airtight container.

Arrabiata Sauce

 SERVES 4

PREP TIME:
15 minutes

COOKING TIME:
30 minutes

nutritional information per serving	518 kcals, 16g fat, 2.5g sat fat, 6g total sugars, trace salt

Serve this tangy hot tomato sauce with pasta shapes, such as penne, or spaghetti. Unlike many other tomato sauce and pasta dishes, it is not traditionally served with grated Parmesan cheese.

INGREDIENTS

150 ml/5 fl oz dry white wine

1 tbsp sun-dried tomato purée

2 fresh red chillies, deseeded and chopped

2 garlic cloves, finely chopped

4 tbsp chopped fresh flat-leaf parsley

salt and pepper

85 g/3 oz pecorino cheese shavings, to garnish

sugocasa

5 tbsp extra virgin olive oil

450 g/1 lb plum tomatoes, chopped

salt and pepper

1. To make the sugocasa. Heat the oil in a frying pan over a high heat until almost smoking. Add the tomatoes and cook, stirring frequently, for 2–3 minutes.

2. Reduce the heat to low and cook gently for 20 minutes, or until very soft. Season to taste with salt and pepper. Press through a non-metallic sieve with a wooden spoon into a saucepan.

3. Add the wine, tomato purée, chillies and garlic to the sugocasa and bring to the boil. Reduce the heat and simmer gently. Check and adjust the seasoning, then stir in the parsley and the cheese. Use as required.

Chipotle Sauce

SERVES 4   PREP TIME: 15 minutes plus soaking time   COOKING TIME: 15 minutes

nutritional information per serving	166 kcals, 16g fat, 1g sat fat, 3g total sugars, trace salt

Smoking jalapeño chillies to make chipotles gives them a delicious depth of flavour but they do remain quite fiery.

INGREDIENTS

2 ancho chillies or to taste, deseeded

1 red pepper

1–2 canned jalapeño or chipotle chillies, drained

5 tbsp pine nuts

juice of ½ lime

2 garlic cloves, roughly chopped

1 tbsp olive oil

salt

1. Put the ancho chillies into a bowl, pour in hot water to cover and leave to soak for 30 minutes. Meanwhile preheat the grill to high.

2. Put the red pepper on a baking sheet and place under the preheated grill, turning occasionally, for about 15 minutes, until charred and blistered. Remove with tongs, put into a polythene bag, tie the top and leave to cool.

3. Drain the ancho chillies, reserving 1 tablespoon of the soaking liquid. Peel, deseed and roughly chop the red pepper.

4. Put the ancho chillies, reserved soaking liquid, red pepper, jalapeño chillies, pine nuts, 1 tablespoon of the lime juice and the garlic into a food processor or blender and process to a smooth paste. With the motor running at low speed, add the oil and process until thoroughly combined. If the sauce is too thick, add a little more lime juice and process briefly again. Season to taste with salt and use as required.

1

2

4

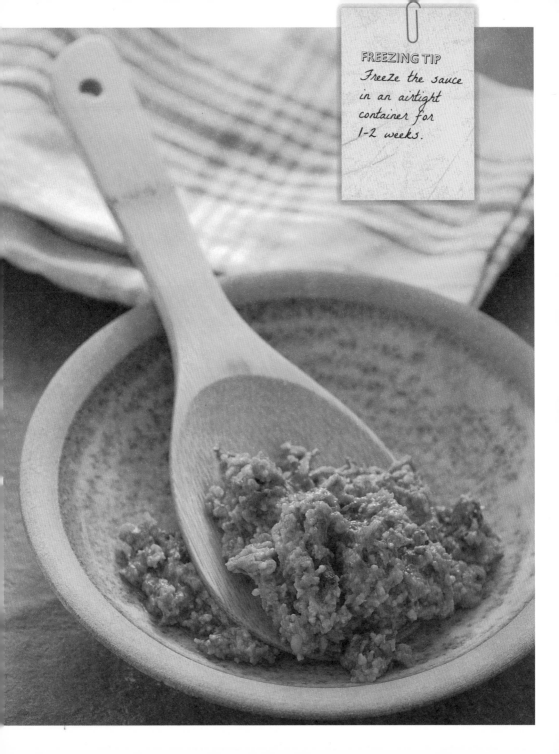

FREEZING TIP
Freeze the sauce
in an airtight
container for
1-2 weeks.

Seafood Sauce

 SERVES 4   PREP TIME: 10 minutes   COOKING TIME: 20–25 minutes

nutritional information per serving	232 kcals, 10g fat, 2g sat fat, 0.2g total sugars, 0.9g salt

This is a great pasta sauce for informal entertaining as it is so quick and easy to make.

INGREDIENTS

675 g/1 lb 8 oz fresh clams, or 280 g/10 oz canned clams, drained

2 tbsp olive oil

2 garlic cloves, finely chopped

400 g/14 oz mixed prepared seafood, such as prawns, squid and mussels, defrosted if frozen

150 ml/5 fl oz white wine

150 ml/5 fl oz fish stock

2 tbsp chopped fresh tarragon

salt and pepper

1. If using fresh clams scrub them clean and discard any that are already open.

2. Heat the oil in a large frying pan. Add the garlic and clams and cook for 2 minutes, shaking the pan to ensure that all of the clams are coated in the oil. Add the remaining seafood to the pan and cook for a further 2 minutes.

3. Pour the wine and stock over the mixed seafood and garlic and bring to the boil. Cover the pan, then lower the heat and simmer for 8–10 minutes, or until the shells open. Discard any clams or mussels that do not open.

4. Stir the tarragon into the sauce and season to taste with salt and pepper. Use as required.

White Wine Sauce

 SERVES 4

 PREP TIME:
10 minutes

 COOKING TIME:
25–30 minutes

nutritional information per serving	844 kcals, 77g fat, 48g sat fat, 4.5g total sugars, 1.2g salt

This rich, creamy sauce goes well with filled pasta such as ravioli – use a stock that matches the filling for extra flavour.

INGREDIENTS

1 onion, chopped

400 ml/14 fl oz dry white wine

1 litre/1¾ pints vegetable, chicken or fish stock

400 ml/14 fl oz double cream

115 g/4 oz butter

3 tbsp finely chopped flat-leaf parsley

salt and pepper

1. Put the onion in a saucepan, pour in the wine and bring to the boil. Cook over a high heat for 10 minutes until the wine has almost completely evaporated.

2. Pour in the stock, bring to the boil and cook for a further 10 minutes, until it has reduced by two-thirds.

3. Stir in the cream and cook for 5 minutes, then stir in the butter, a little at a time. Add the parsley, season to taste with salt and pepper and use as required.

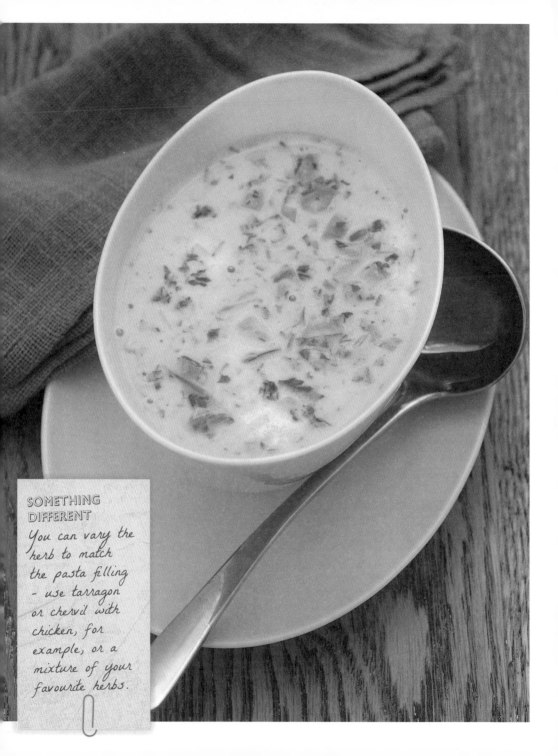

Index